SPECIAL REQUESTS

Editor
Judith Evans

Photo Editor
Larry Coyne

Cover Photographer
Jerry Naunheim Jr.

Photo Toning
Hillary Levin

Administrative Assistance
Annette Reavling

Art Direction/Design
Tom Borgman

Copy Editor
Babette Morgan

Research
Mike Meiners
Mark Learman
Matthew Fernandes

Sales and Marketing
Gail LaFata

ISBN-10: 0-9661397-8-X

ISBN-13: 978-0-9661397-8-5

Printed by Walsworth Publishing Co., Marceline, Mo.

To order additional copies, call **1-800-329-0224**.   Order online at **www.post-dispatchstore.com**

SPECIAL REQUESTS

100 favorite restaurant recipes
from the pages of the St. Louis Post-Dispatch

SNACKS, STARTERS, SAUCES AND DRESSINGS

MAIN DISHES

ON THE SIDE

DESERTS

ACKNOWLEDGMENTS

Chefs cook by adding a splash of this, a dash of that and a handful of something else. Transforming those less-than-specific (and often, less-than-accurate) directions into the tested, reliable recipes printed here was no easy task.

I began writing the Special Request column in 1996 with the help of home economist Madie Stroud, who adapted and developed the recipes for home kitchens. Babette Morgan (who also copy-edited this book) took over the writing and recipe development in 1999, followed by freelance writer Mary Billings and her late husband, Jack, in late 2000. The ongoing success of the column is a testament to their excellent work.

Judith Evans
Food Editor
St. Louis Post-Dispatch

INTRODUCTION

Over the past decade, hundreds of local chefs generously have shared recipes sought by the readers of "Special Request," a column that appears each Wednesday in the St. Louis Post-Dispatch. We've gathered 100 favorites here, all tested and adapted for home kitchens.

You'll find pasta galore, fitting for a city known for its Italian restaurants. Readers love to replicate restaurant soups at home, so we've included a wide array. Ethnic restaurants thrive in our area, and you'll find specialties from many nations in these pages.

Sadly, a few of the restaurants represented here are no longer in business. But their recipes live on.

Whether you cook for family, friends or a restaurant full of customers, food is for sharing. Enjoy!

SNACKS, STARTERS, SAUCES AND DRESSINGS

Blue Cheese Soufflé • Crostini with Spanakopita • Spinach-Artichoke Dip •
David Slay's Original Crispy Fried Spinach • Pan-Fried Green Olives Stuffed with
Sausage and Herbed Goat Cheese • Mangia Wings in Cayenne Honey Sauce •
Mango Salsa • Dock Salsa • Jerk Chile Mayo • Pesto Sauce • Grilled Portobellos •
Balsamic Roasted Portobello with Brie • Skillet Cornbread with Rock Shrimp •
Shrimp Sambuca • Chilled Cucumber and Dill Soup • Corn Chowder • Roasted
Butternut Squash Bisque with Wild Rice and Crème Anise • Kabocha Pumpkin Soup •
Roasted Red Pepper Bisque • Wicklow Salad • Mayfair Salad Dressing

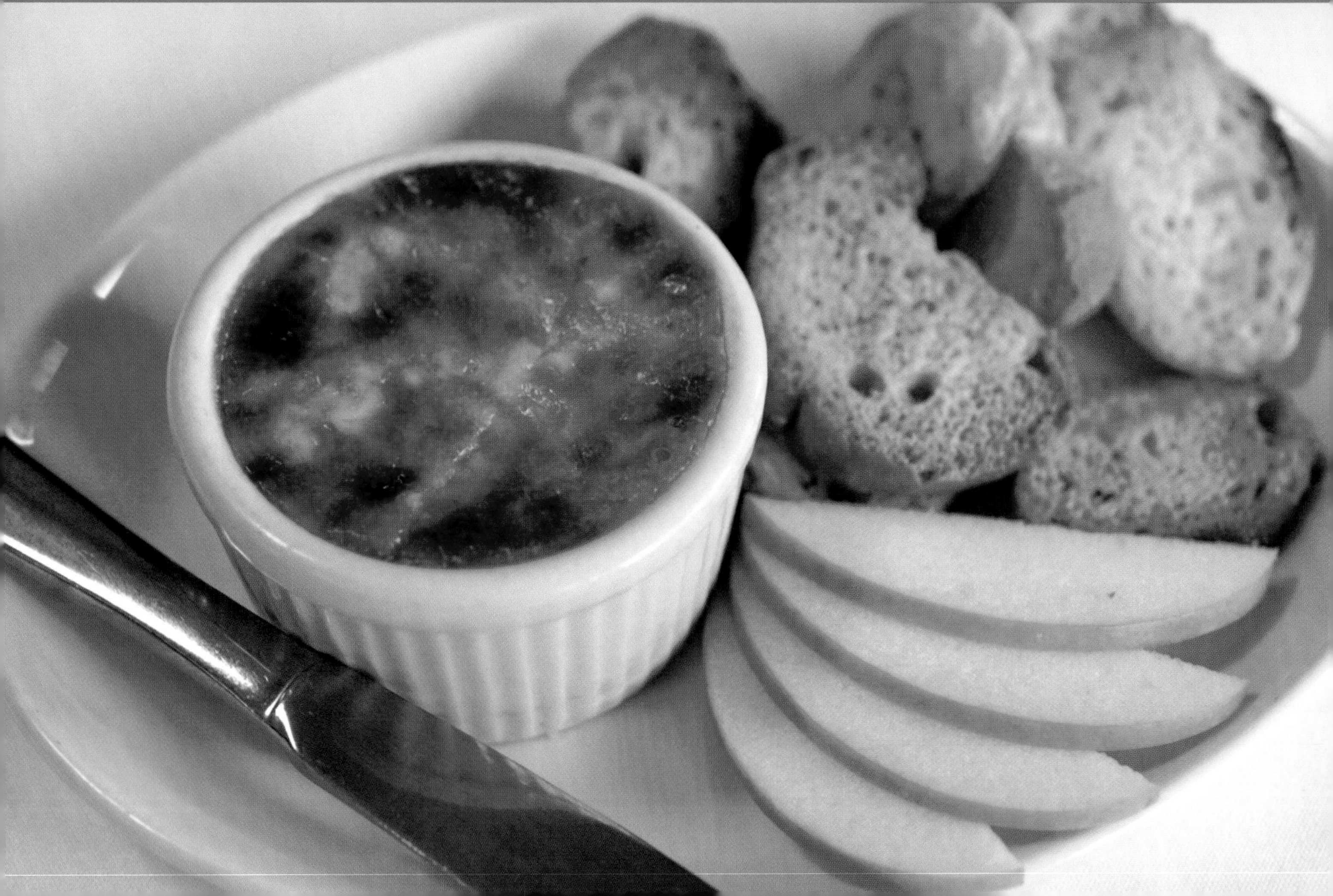

BLUE CHEESE SOUFFLÉ

Yield: About 16 servings

1 egg, lightly beaten

¼ cup milk

1 cup mayonnaise

1 cup finely crumbled blue cheese

1 cup grated Cheddar cheese

1 cup diced onion

¼ teaspoon salt or to taste

¼ teaspoon ground pepper or to taste

Preheat oven to 300 degrees. Stir together egg, milk, mayonnaise, cheeses, onion, salt and pepper. Transfer to an 8-inch-square glass or ceramic baking dish. Place the baking dish in a roasting pan; place in the oven, then pour hot water into the roasting pan. The water should come halfway up the sides of the baking dish. Bake 45 minutes or until the soufflé is set on top and lightly browned. Serve hot with crusty bread or crackers.

Note: The Crossing delivers this complimentary appetizer to each table in individual 3- to 4-ounce ramekins.

PER SERVING

Calories 170 • fat 16.5g • % calories from fat 87 • saturated fat 5g • cholesterol 34mg • protein 4g • carbohydrate 1.5g • sugar 1g • fiber 0 • sodium 280mg • calcium 104mg • potassium 53mg

13

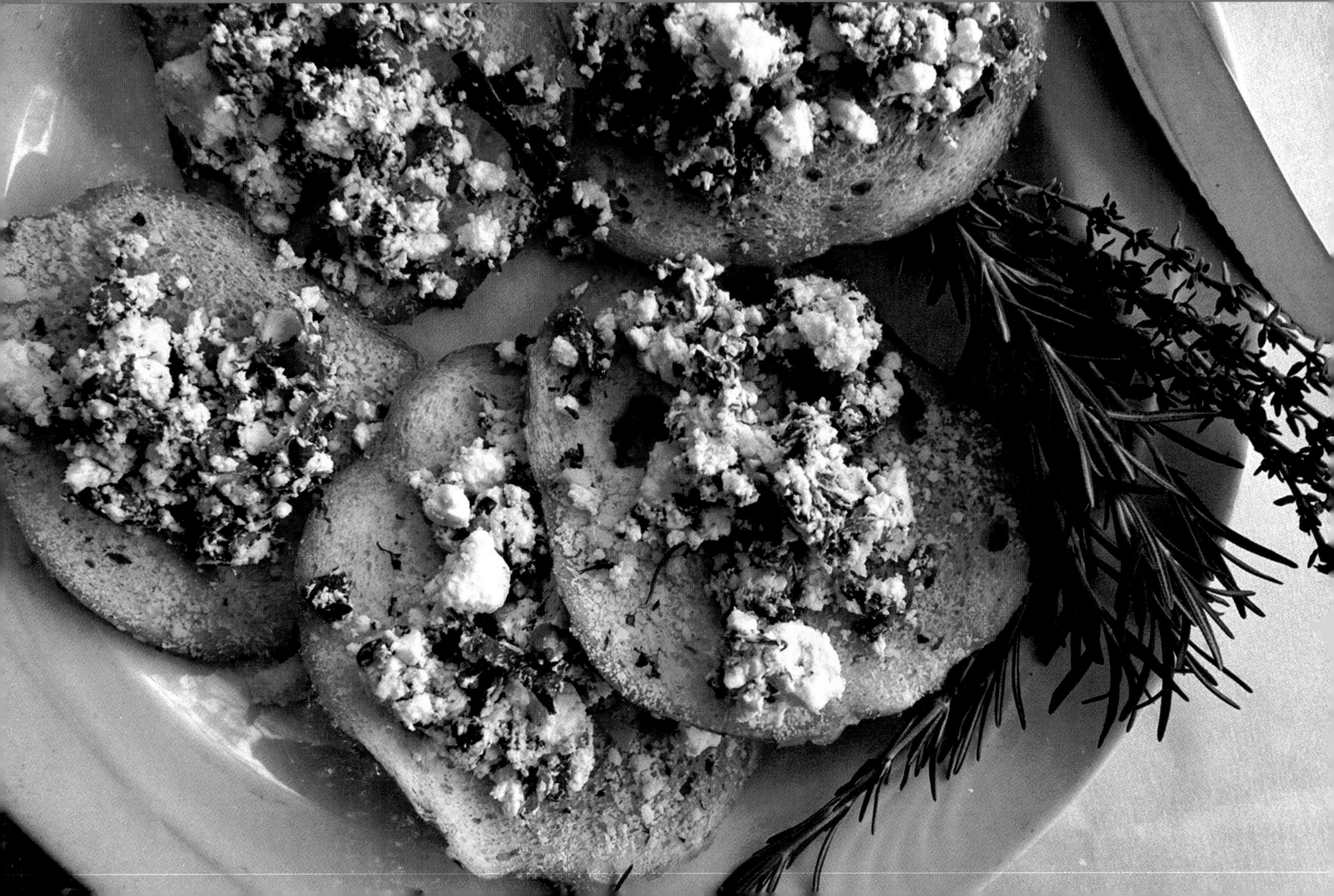

CROSTINI WITH SPANAKOPITA

Yield: 12 servings

FOR CROSTINI:

½ cup (1 stick) butter

24 very thin slices French bread (about ½ loaf)

1 tablespoon minced fresh garlic

Freshly ground white pepper

½ cup grated Parmesan cheese

FOR SPANAKOPITA:

2 ounces fresh spinach

4 ounces feta cheese

2 ounces cream cheese, at room temperature

1½ tablespoons pine nuts, roughly chopped

1 pinch freshly ground white pepper

1 pinch granulated garlic or garlic powder

To prepare crostini: Preheat oven to 350 degrees.

Melt butter over medium heat. Remove from heat; let sit until milky solids sink to the bottom of the pan. Skim off the golden melted butter from the top. Discard the milky solids.

Spread bread slices on a cookie sheet. Combine melted butter and garlic. Add pepper to taste. Brush on bread slices. Bake for 10 minutes or until slightly crisp. Sprinkle with Parmesan cheese. Return to the oven until cheese melts, about 1 minute. Let cool.

To prepare spanakopita: Plunge spinach into a large pot of boiling water; cook just until tender. Transfer to a bowl of ice water, then drain. Squeeze spinach dry; chop coarsely.

Combine feta cheese, cream cheese, pine nuts, spinach, white pepper and granulated garlic in a medium bowl. Mix well with hands. Spoon spinach mixture on the crostini. Return to oven until warm, about 3 minutes. Serve warm.

PER SERVING
calories 313 · fat 13.5g · % calories from fat 39 · saturated fat 8g · cholesterol 37mg · protein 11g · carbohydrate 37g · sugar 2g · fiber 2g · sodium 590mg · calcium 122mg · potassium 133mg

GROWLERS PUB 3811 S. Lindbergh Blvd. • Sunset Hills, Mo. • 314-984-9009 • 763 Old Ballas Rd. • Creve Coeur, Mo. • 314-432-3110 • www.growlerspub.com

SPINACH-ARTICHOKE DIP

Yield: About 3 cups

1 tablespoon plus ¾ teaspoon vegetable oil

2 tablespoons diced yellow onion
(cut into ¼-inch pieces)

⅛ teaspoon minced garlic

Nonstick cooking spray

6 tablespoons chicken broth

¼ teaspoon granulated sugar

6 tablespoons heavy cream

1 cup chopped artichoke hearts

2 packed tablespoons frozen chopped
spinach, thawed and squeezed dry

3 tablespoons sour cream

⅛ teaspoon Tabasco-brand pepper sauce

¼ teaspoon salt

1⅛ teaspoons lemon juice

¼ cup grated Parmesan cheese

1¼ cups shredded Monterey Jack cheese

1 tablespoon butter

1 tablespoon all-purpose flour

Heat oil in a sauté pan over medium-high heat. Add onion and garlic; sauté until onion is transparent.

Coat the inside of the top half of a 1½-quart double boiler with nonstick cooking spray.

Transfer sautéed vegetables to the double boiler. Stir in broth, sugar, cream, artichoke hearts, spinach, sour cream, Tabasco, salt, lemon juice and cheeses.

Cook, stirring occasionally and scraping the sides of the pot with a spatula, until cheese is completely melted.

Melt butter in a sauté pan; whisk in flour to make a roux. Cook, stirring, until dark brown (do not let burn). Stir roux into cheese mixture. Cook until mixture begins to thicken. Remove from heat.

Serve dip warm with corn chips or pita bread.

PER (¼-CUP) SERVING
calories 116 • fat 10g • % calories from fat 78 • saturated fat 5.5g • cholesterol 26mg • protein 4g • carbohydrate 2.5g • sugar 0 • fiber 0 • sodium 217mg • calcium 119mg • potassium 33mg

ZUZU'S PETALS was located in Kirkwood, Mo.

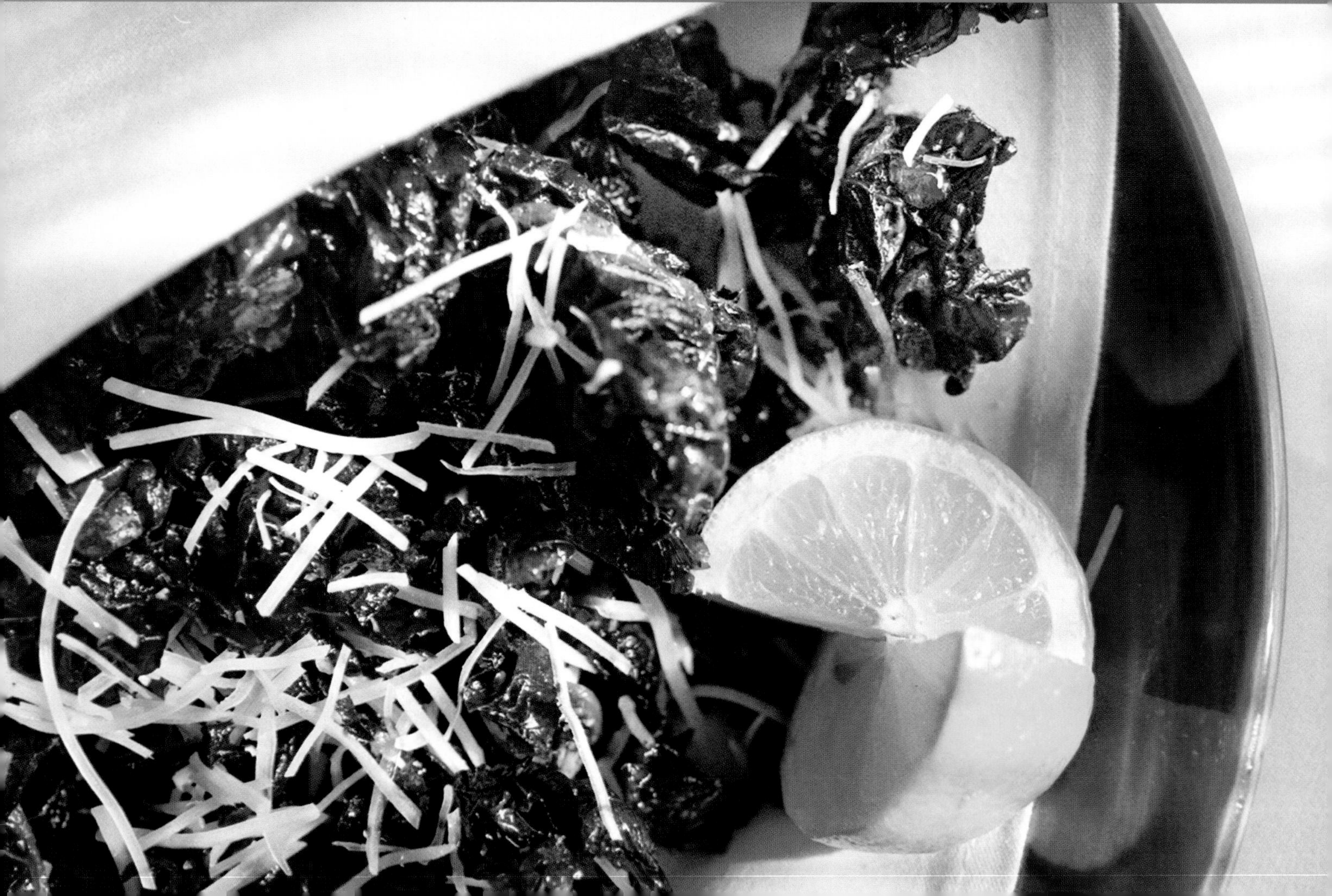

DAVID SLAY'S ORIGINAL CRISPY FRIED SPINACH

Yield: 3 servings

1 pound fresh spinach

**About 1 quart canola or
vegetable oil**

**1 tablespoon grated
Parmesan cheese**

1 pinch salt

**Juice of ½ lemon
(1 to 2 tablespoons)**

Quickly rinse spinach several times; drain well.

Pour 2 to 3 inches of oil into a large pot, electric fryer or wok; heat oil to 400 degrees. Add spinach in batches that fit comfortably in the pot. Using a slotted spoon or Chinese strainer to keep the spinach submerged, cook about 2 minutes, until spinach turns very dark green. Remove with the slotted spoon or strainer, and gently lay spinach on paper towels to drain excess oil.

Put spinach in a bowl; toss with Parmesan, salt and lemon juice. Serve on a napkin folded to fit a plate.

Notes: Have the lemon juice, salt and Parmesan ready before you fry the spinach, then toss and serve immediately.

This dish was a favorite at previous restaurants owned by David Slay, starting in 1980 at Café Hampton.

PER SERVING
calories 98 • fat 6g • % calories from fat 55 • saturated fat 1g • cholesterol 2mg • protein 5g • carbohydrate 6g • sugar 1g • fiber 3g • sodium 145mg • calcium 169mg • potassium 855mg

PAN-FRIED GREEN OLIVES STUFFED WITH SAUSAGE AND HERBED GOAT CHEESE

Yield: 6 servings

FOR FILLING:

½ teaspoon olive oil

¼ pound spicy Italian sausage

1 clove garlic, minced

2 tablespoons finely diced white onion

¼ cup plus 2 tablespoons goat cheese

1½ teaspoons finely chopped fresh parsley

½ teaspoon finely chopped fresh oregano

¼ cup fresh bread crumbs

FOR OLIVES:

35 to 40 jumbo pitted brine-cured green olives

⅓ cup all-purpose flour

2 eggs, beaten

1¼ cups fresh bread crumbs

Olive oil, for frying

To prepare filling: Heat oil in a medium skillet over medium-high heat. Crumble sausage into skillet. Add garlic and onion; stir to combine. Cook until sausage has browned, about 5 minutes. Drain if necessary, let cool, and chop fine. Add goat cheese, parsley, oregano and bread crumbs; mix well.

To stuff and fry olives: Pinch off about ½ teaspoon filling; form into a cylinder slightly smaller than the olive cavity. Fill olive, using a chopstick to pack firmly; repeat with remaining olives.

Place flour, eggs and bread crumbs in separate shallow bowls. Roll olives in flour, dip into eggs and then roll in bread crumbs. Refrigerate for at least 30 minutes. (Do not skip this step. Chilling gives the breading time to bind.)

Pour oil into a medium skillet to a depth of ¼ to ⅓ inch; place over medium-high heat. When oil begins to shimmer, but before it begins to smoke, add olives in small batches. Cook until breading is golden brown, about 1 minute on each side. Drain on paper towels.

Tester's note: The olives we used were about 1¼ inches long and 1 inch across. This recipe makes 1 cup of filling. Leftover filling can be used to stuff chicken breasts or tomatoes.

PER SERVING

calories 259 • fat 21g • % calories from fat 73 • saturated fat 4g • cholesterol 75mg • protein 5.5g • carbohydrate 12g • sugar 1g • fiber 2g • sodium 743mg • calcium 54mg • potassium 71mg

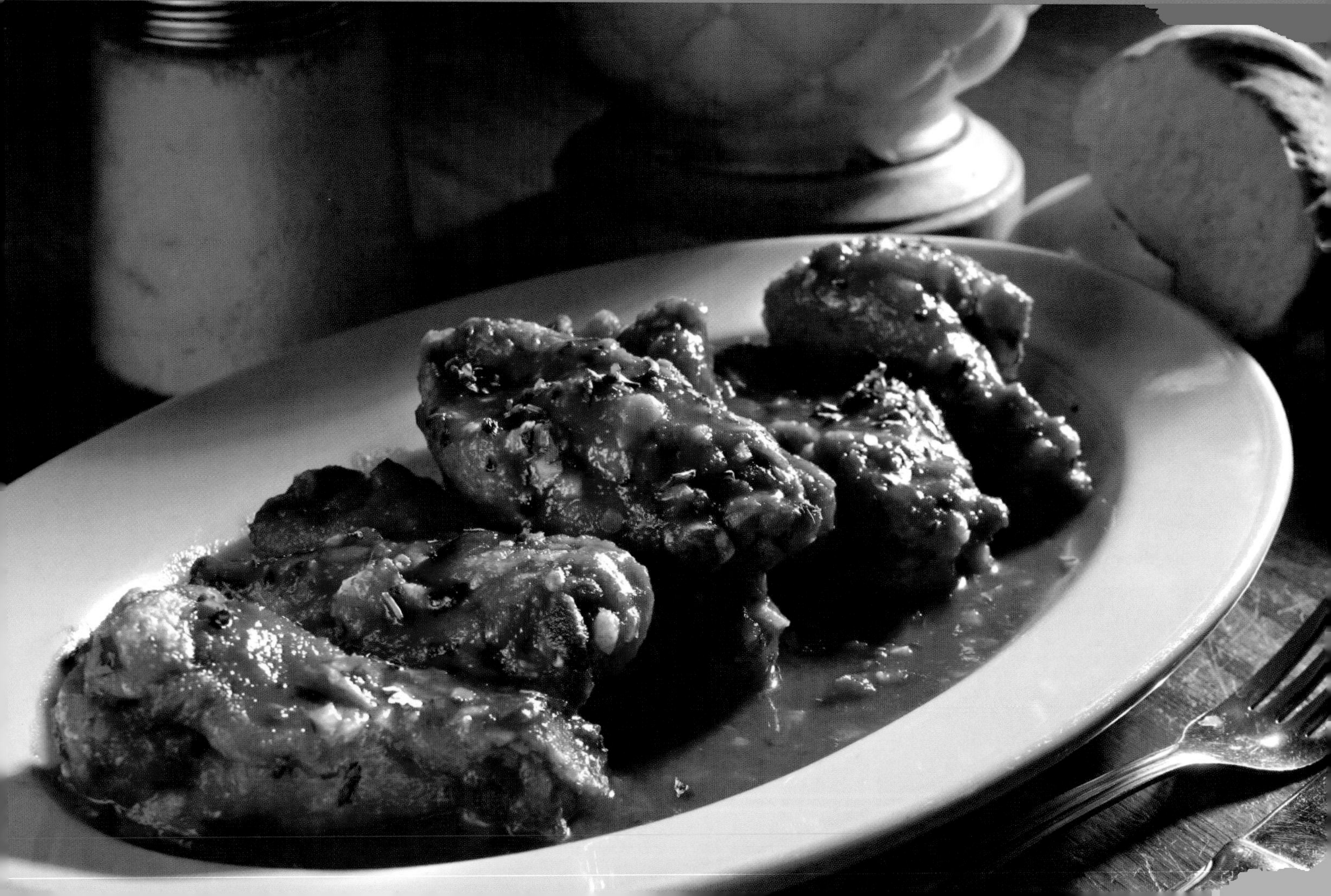

MANGIA WINGS IN CAYENNE HONEY SAUCE

Yield: 2 to 10 servings

1 cup Frank's hot sauce

2 tablespoons butter

¼ cup honey

1 tablespoon red-pepper flakes

2 tablespoons finely minced garlic

½ rounded teaspoon ground cumin

½ rounded teaspoon dried oregano

½ rounded teaspoon dried basil

½ rounded teaspoon dried thyme

½ rounded teaspoon Madras curry powder

½ rounded teaspoon ground red (cayenne) pepper

1 to 5 pounds chicken wings (see note)

Vegetable oil, for deep-frying

Combine hot sauce, butter, honey, red-pepper flakes, garlic, cumin, oregano, basil, thyme, curry powder and cayenne in a small saucepan; cook over medium heat, stirring often, until butter is melted and incorporated into the sauce. Let cool.

Cut each wing into 3 pieces at joints; discard wing tips. Heat oil for deep-frying. Fry chicken; drain well. Place sauce in a bowl, add chicken and toss to coat well. Remove chicken from sauce. Serve warm or well chilled, with excess sauce for dipping.

Note: This recipe makes enough sauce for 2 servings of wings as Mangia Italiano presents them. For wings without a lot of extra sauce, this recipe will coat 4 to 5 pounds of chicken wings.

PER SERVING (based on 2 servings, including all the sauce)
calories 697 • fat 41g • % calories from fat 53 • saturated fat 14g • cholesterol 142mg • protein 32g • carbohydrate 51g • sugar 38g • fiber 2.5g • sodium 4,866mg • calcium 62mg • potassium 382mg

PER SERVING (based on 10 servings, made with 5 pounds wings, including all the sauce)
calories 370 • fat 23g • % calories from fat 56 • saturated fat 7g • cholesterol 118mg • protein 30.5g • carbohydrate 10g • sugar 7.5g • fiber 0.5g • sodium 1,054mg • calcium 24mg • potassium 290mg

MANGO SALSA

Yield: 3 cups

2 ripe mangoes

3/4 teaspoon sambal oelek (Asian chile paste; see note)

1 jalapeño, stemmed and chopped, or more to taste

1 yellow onion, chopped

1 tablespoon dry mustard

1 tablespoon vegetable oil

3/4 cup rice vinegar

1/2 teaspoon ground turmeric

3/4 teaspoon curry powder

1/4 teaspoon ground cloves

3/4 teaspoon kosher salt

1/4 cup water

Cut each side from mangoes. Slip a large spoon between pulp and peel. Scoop out pulp; cut into 1-inch cubes.

In a food processor or blender, combine mango cubes, sambal oelek, jalapeño and onion. Add mustard, oil and vinegar; process until smooth.

Transfer mixture to a saucepan. Add turmeric, curry powder, cloves, salt and water. Bring to a boil over medium heat, then reduce heat and simmer until thickened, about 15 minutes. Let cool, then refrigerate. Serve with skewers of grilled chicken or shrimp.

Salsa keeps up to 3 weeks in refrigerator. Recipe may be doubled.

Note: Sambal oelek is a ground chile paste, with or without garlic added. It is available in Asian markets and many local grocery stores.

PER (2-TABLESPOON) SERVING
calories 21 • fat 0.5g • % calories from fat 21 • saturated fat 0 • cholesterol 0 • protein 0.5g • carbohydrate 3.5g • sugar 3g • fiber 0.5g • sodium 62mg • calcium 4mg • potassium 37.5mg

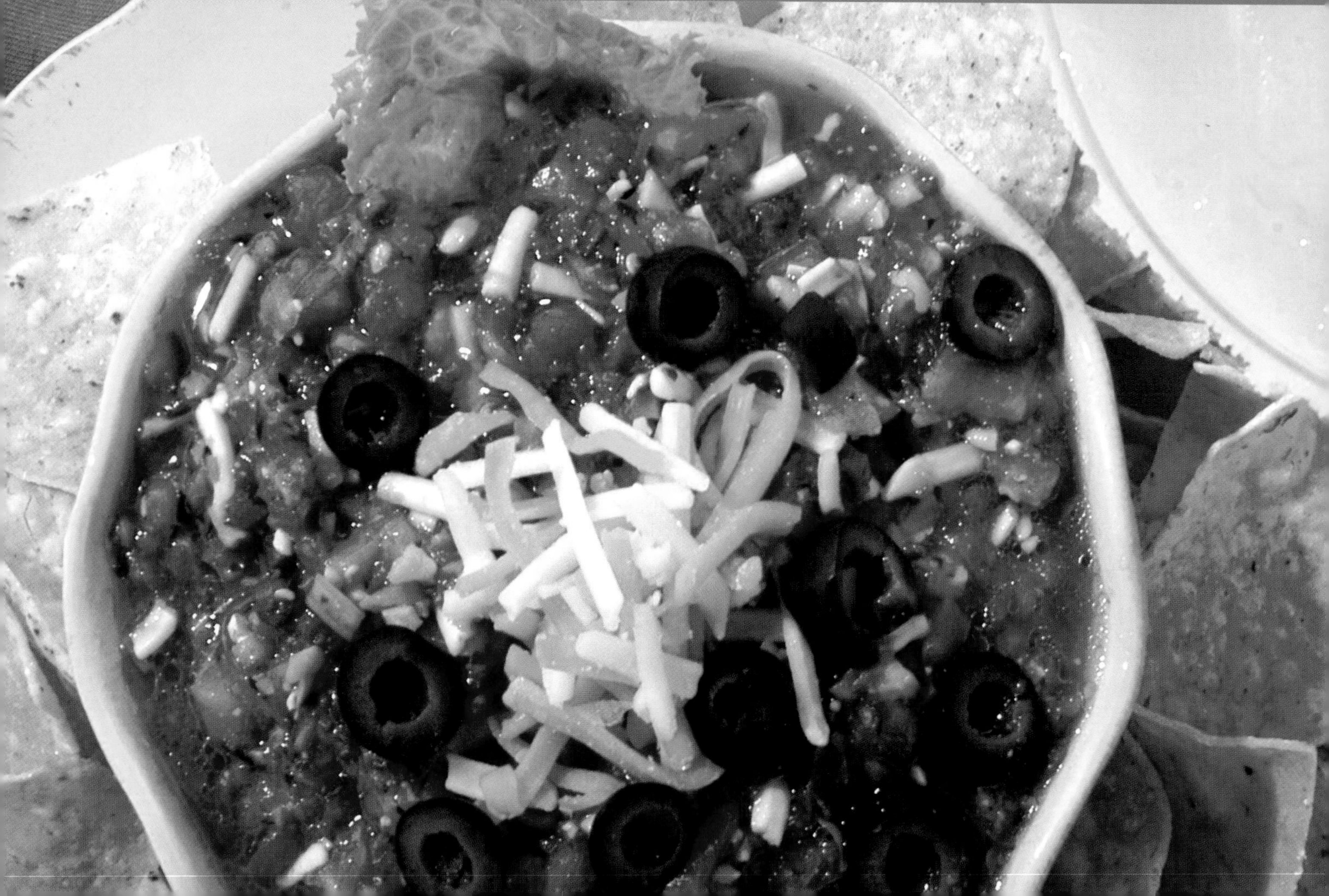

DOCK SALSA

Yield: About 2½ cups salsa; 6 to 8 servings

1 (0.7-ounce) packet Good Seasons Italian dressing mix

⅓ cup vinegar

½ cup vegetable oil

4 ounces shredded Cheddar cheese

4 ounces shredded mozzarella cheese

1 (4-ounce) can chopped green chiles

1 (4-ounce) can chopped black olives or ½ cup pitted black olives, chopped

3 green onions, chopped

1 ripe tomato, chopped

1 (8-ounce) package tortilla chips

Combine dressing mix, vinegar and oil as directed on the dressing mix packet. Set aside.

In a 2-quart bowl, combine cheeses, chiles, olives, green onions and tomato. Add dressing; stir gently to combine. Serve with tortilla chips.

PER SERVING (based on 8 servings, including chips)
calories 392 • fat 28g • % calories from fat 64 • saturated fat 8g • cholesterol 24mg • protein 9g • carbohydrate 26g • sugar 3g • fiber 3g • sodium 816mg • calcium 269mg • potassium 201mg

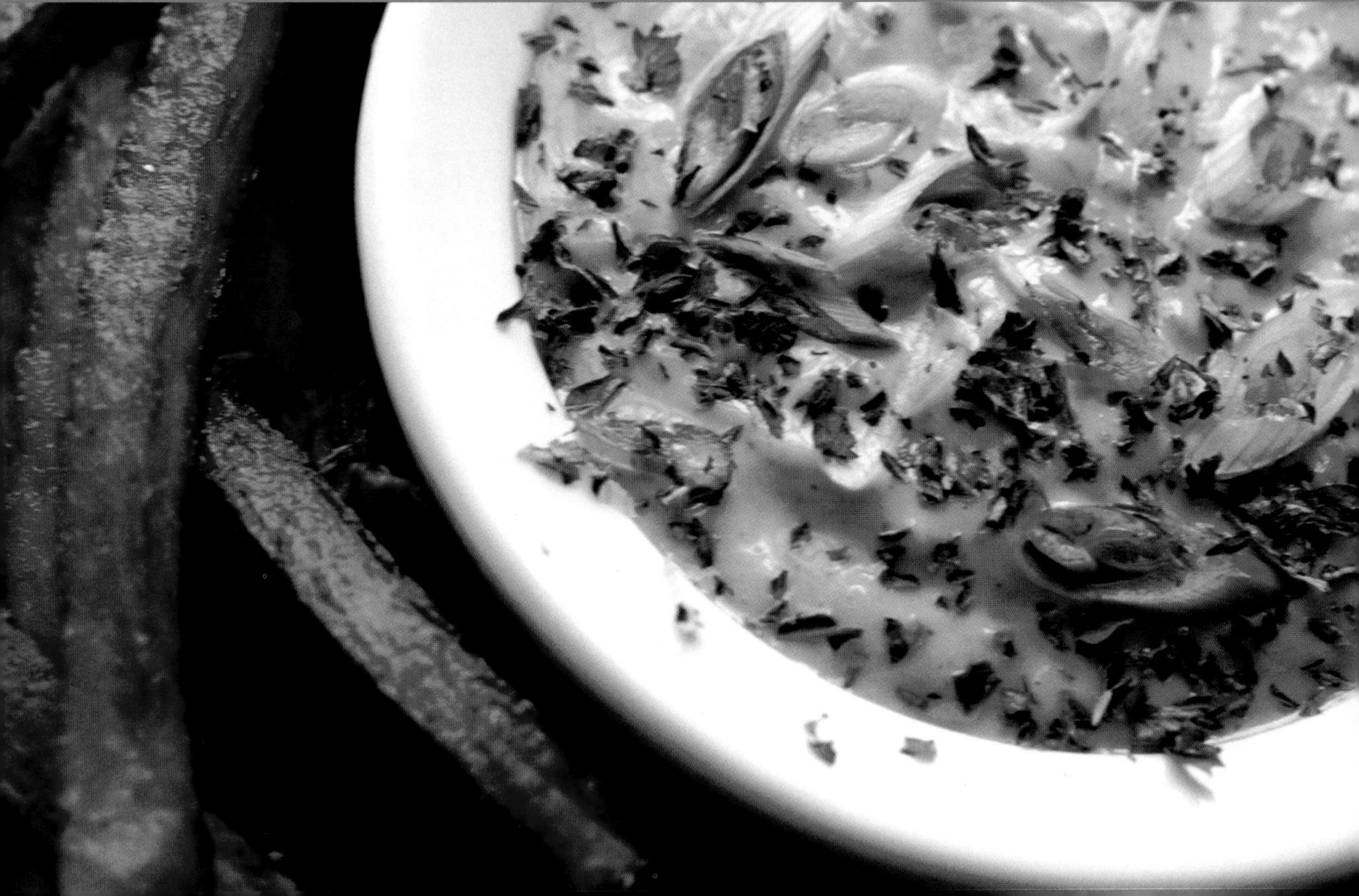

JERK CHILE MAYO

Yield: About 3 cups

**2¹/₂ cups mayonnaise
(such as Hellmann's)**

**2¹/₂ tablespoons chile garlic
sauce (see note)**

**1¹/₂ tablespoons Caribbean
jerk seasoning**

**¹/₂ tablespoon jarred minced
garlic packed in oil**

4 dashes Tabasco sauce

**Chopped fresh tarragon,
for optional garnish**

Combine mayonnaise, chile garlic sauce, jerk seasoning, minced garlic and Tabasco in a medium bowl. Mix well. Refrigerate in a covered container. Just before serving, garnish with chopped fresh tarragon.

Note: Chile garlic sauce can be found in Asian markets.

PER TABLESPOON
calories 81 · fat 9g · % calories from fat 100 · saturated fat 1g · cholesterol 4mg · protein 0 · carbohydrate 0 · sugar 0 · fiber 0 · sodium 125mg · calcium 0 · potassium 0

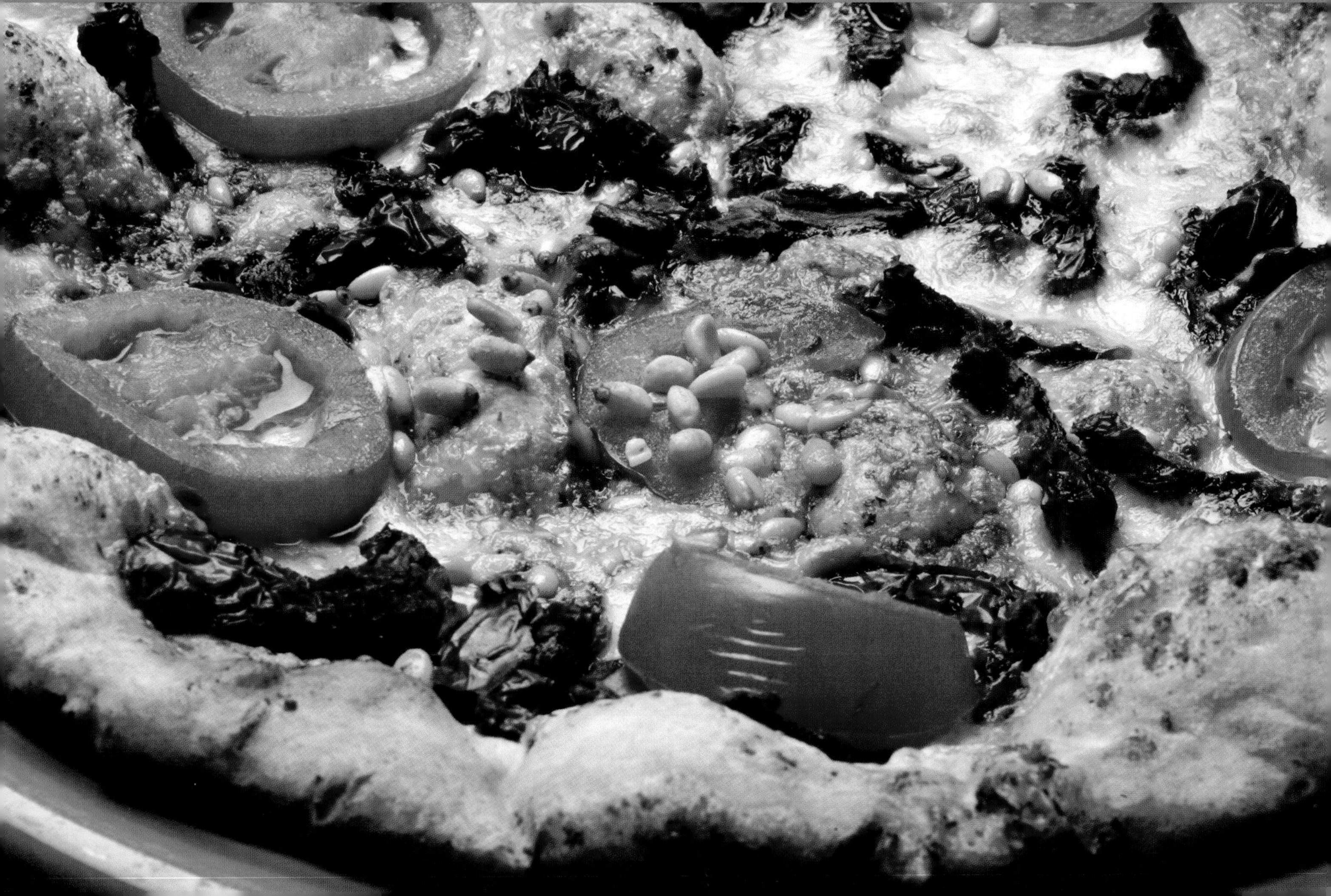

PESTO SAUCE

Yield: 2 cups

¼ cup garlic cloves

⅓ cup walnuts

⅓ cup grated Parmesan cheese

5 ounces basil leaves (about 8 cups loosely packed)

1 cup olive oil

1 teaspoon salt

1 teaspoon ground black pepper

1 tablespoon lemon juice

Combine garlic and walnuts in the work bowl of a food processor; process until finely chopped. Add Parmesan and basil leaves (in batches if necessary, depending on the capacity of your processor); process until puréed, scraping bowl as needed. With machine running, gradually drizzle in olive oil to make a thick paste. Add salt, pepper and lemon juice; pulse to combine.

Use as a topping for pizza or with pasta.

Note: Refrigerate leftovers for a day or two in a clean container, covering surface with additional olive oil to prevent discoloration. Freeze for longer storage.

PER TABLESPOON

calories 80 • fat 8g • % calories from fat 90 • saturated fat 1g • cholesterol 1mg • protein 1g • carbohydrate 1g • sugar 0 • fiber 0 • sodium 95mg • calcium 25mg • potassium 30mg

GRILLED PORTOBELLOS

Yield: 4 servings.

¼ cup white wine

¼ cup olive oil

2 cloves garlic, minced

½ teaspoon dried oregano

Salt

Ground black pepper

½ cup balsamic vinegar, divided

4 large portobello mushrooms, stems removed

Prepare a medium fire in the grill. Meanwhile, in a shallow bowl, whisk together wine, oil, garlic, oregano, salt and pepper to taste and ¼ cup vinegar. Add mushrooms; marinate for about 15 minutes. Grill over medium heat until soft, about 5 minutes per side.

Pour the remaining ¼ cup balsamic vinegar in a small saucepan; simmer over medium heat about 5 minutes, until it reaches the consistency of syrup; drizzle over grilled mushrooms.

PER SERVING

calories 97 • fat 5g • % calories from fat 46 • saturated fat 0.5g • cholesterol 0 • protein 2g • carbohydrate 10g • sugar 7g • fiber 1g • sodium 313mg • calcium 9mg • potassium 424mg

BALSAMIC ROASTED PORTOBELLO WITH BRIE

Yield: 6 servings

2 tablespoons chopped garlic

2 sprigs fresh thyme, chopped

2 tablespoons granulated sugar

¼ cup olive oil

1 cup balsamic vinegar, divided

6 portobello mushroom caps, each about 3 inches in diameter, gills removed

12 ounces brie cheese

Salt

Freshly cracked black pepper

6 cups baby greens (mesclun mix)

4 to 6 tablespoons Italian salad dressing

Shaved Asiago cheese, for garnish

Combine garlic, thyme, sugar, oil and ¼ cup vinegar in a bowl or self-sealing plastic bag. Add mushroom caps; toss gently to coat with marinade. Marinate at least 1 hour or refrigerate up to 24 hours.

Place remaining ¾ cup balsamic vinegar in a small pot; cook over medium heat until reduced to 2 tablespoons, about 15 minutes. Set aside.

Preheat oven to 375 degrees. Remove mushrooms from marinade; fill caps with brie. Season lightly with salt and pepper. Bake 10 to 12 minutes or until cheese is bubbling.

Place each mushroom in the center of a small plate. Toss greens with dressing. Spoon dressed greens over cheese-filled mushrooms. Drizzle with balsamic syrup; top with Asiago.

PER SERVING
calories 329 • fat 25g • % calories from fat 68 • saturated fat 11g • cholesterol 57mg • protein 15g • carbohydrate 11g • sugar 6.5g • fiber 2.5g • sodium 456mg • calcium 149mg • potassium 683mg

SKILLET CORNBREAD WITH ROCK SHRIMP

Yield: About 8 servings (16 cornbread cakes)

FOR SORGHUM BUTTER:

1 cup (2 sticks) butter, softened

2 tablespoons sorghum molasses

FOR CORNBREAD:

1⅓ cups frozen corn kernels, thawed, divided

1⅓ cups all-purpose flour

⅔ cup cornmeal

2 tablespoons baking powder

⅓ cup granulated sugar

2 eggs, beaten

2 cups buttermilk

3 tablespoons vegetable oil

2½ teaspoons ground cumin

2 teaspoons salt

1 pinch ground red (cayenne) pepper

⅓ cup sliced green onions

⅓ cup minced red onion

1 tablespoon seeded, minced jalapeño

⅓ cup chopped fresh cilantro

1 cup coarsely chopped peeled and deveined rock shrimp

Butter

Whole cooked shrimp or rock shrimp, for optional garnish

To prepare sorghum butter: Combine butter and molasses; beat until thoroughly combined. Set aside.

To prepare cornbread: In a food processor or blender, purée ⅔ cup corn; set aside.

Sift flour, cornmeal, baking powder and sugar together into a medium bowl; set aside. Combine eggs, buttermilk and oil; mix until well blended. Stir in flour mixture. Stir in puréed corn, remaining ⅔ cup corn kernels, cumin, salt, cayenne, green onions, red onion, jalapeño, cilantro and chopped shrimp.

Preheat a griddle or skillet over medium-low heat; add enough butter to lightly coat the surface (see note). Ladle ⅓ cup batter onto skillet, much like a pancake. Shake the skillet slightly to level the batter for even cooking. Cook until lightly browned, 7 to 8 minutes, then turn and cook 5 to 6 minutes more, until lightly browned.

To serve, top with dollop of sorghum butter. If desired, garnish with whole cooked shrimp or rock shrimp.

Note: Using more butter in the skillet, almost to the point of frying, will result in a crispy-edged cake, a desirable effect for texture and flavor.

PER SERVING
calories 517 • fat 31g • % calories from fat 54 • saturated fat 16g • cholesterol 157mg • protein 13.5g • carbohydrate 46g • sugar 14g • fiber 2.5g • sodium 1,022mg • calcium 338mg • potassium 419mg

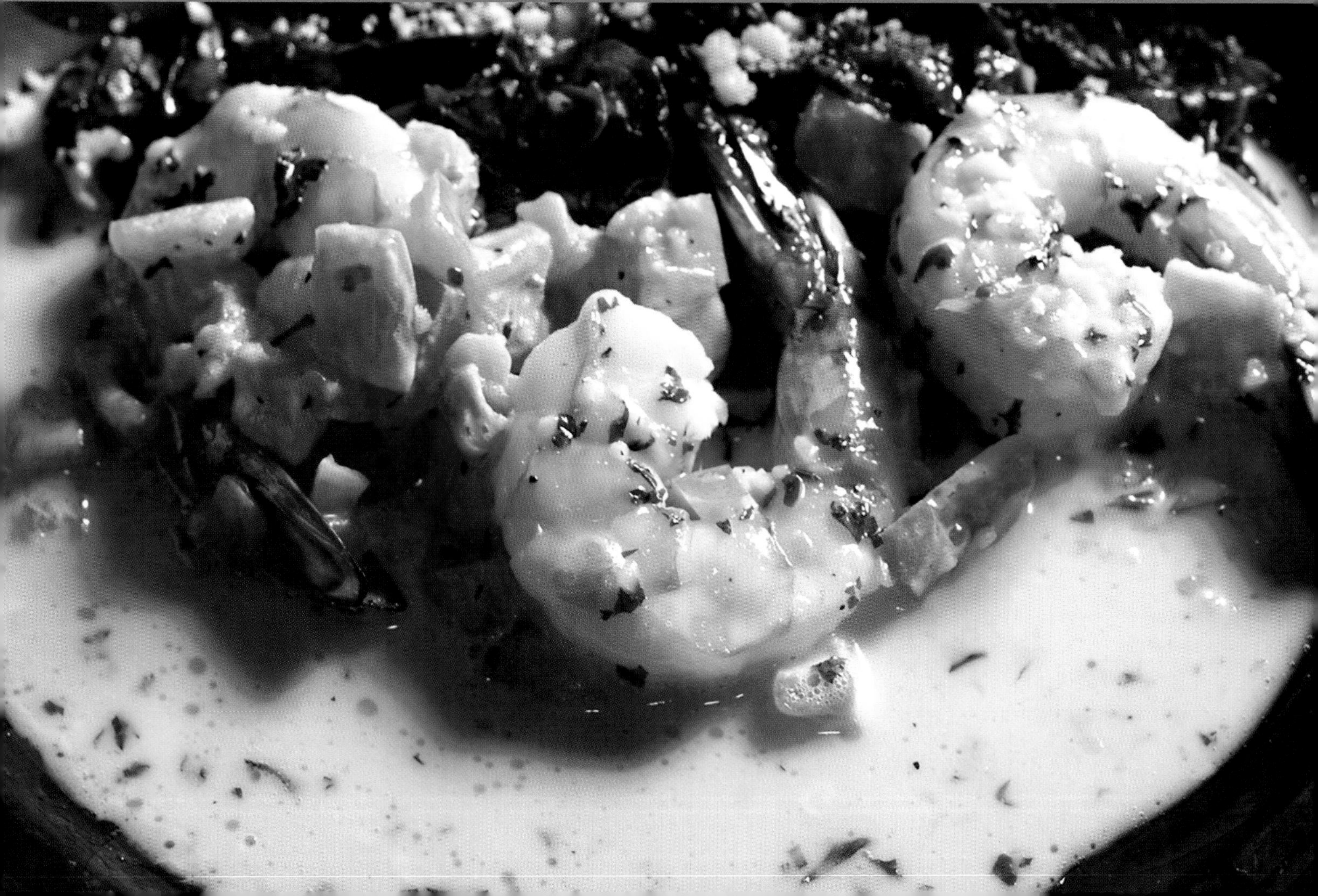

SHRIMP SAMBUCA

Yield: 1 serving (see note)

4 large shrimp

Extra-virgin olive oil

1/3 cup seeded diced tomatoes

1/2 teaspoon minced fresh garlic

1 pinch dried red pepper flakes

Salt

Ground black pepper

2 tablespoons warm Sambuca or to taste

6 tablespoons heavy cream

1 teaspoon chopped fresh parsley

Peel shrimp, leaving last shell section and tail intact; devein. Film a medium skillet with olive oil; sauté shrimp with tomatoes, garlic and pepper flakes until shrimp are half done, about 1½ minutes. Season to taste with salt and pepper.

Add Sambuca; carefully touch a lighted match to the Sambuca. When flame subsides, add cream. Cook over medium heat until sauce is slightly thickened, about 3 minutes; stir in parsley. Arrange shrimp and sauce on plate. Serve immediately with crusty bread.

Note: This recipe can be doubled.

PER SERVING
calories 394 • fat 38.5g • % calories from fat 88 • saturated fat 21g • cholesterol 159mg • protein 7.5g • carbohydrate 7g • sugar 4g • fiber 1g • sodium 76mg • calcium 78mg

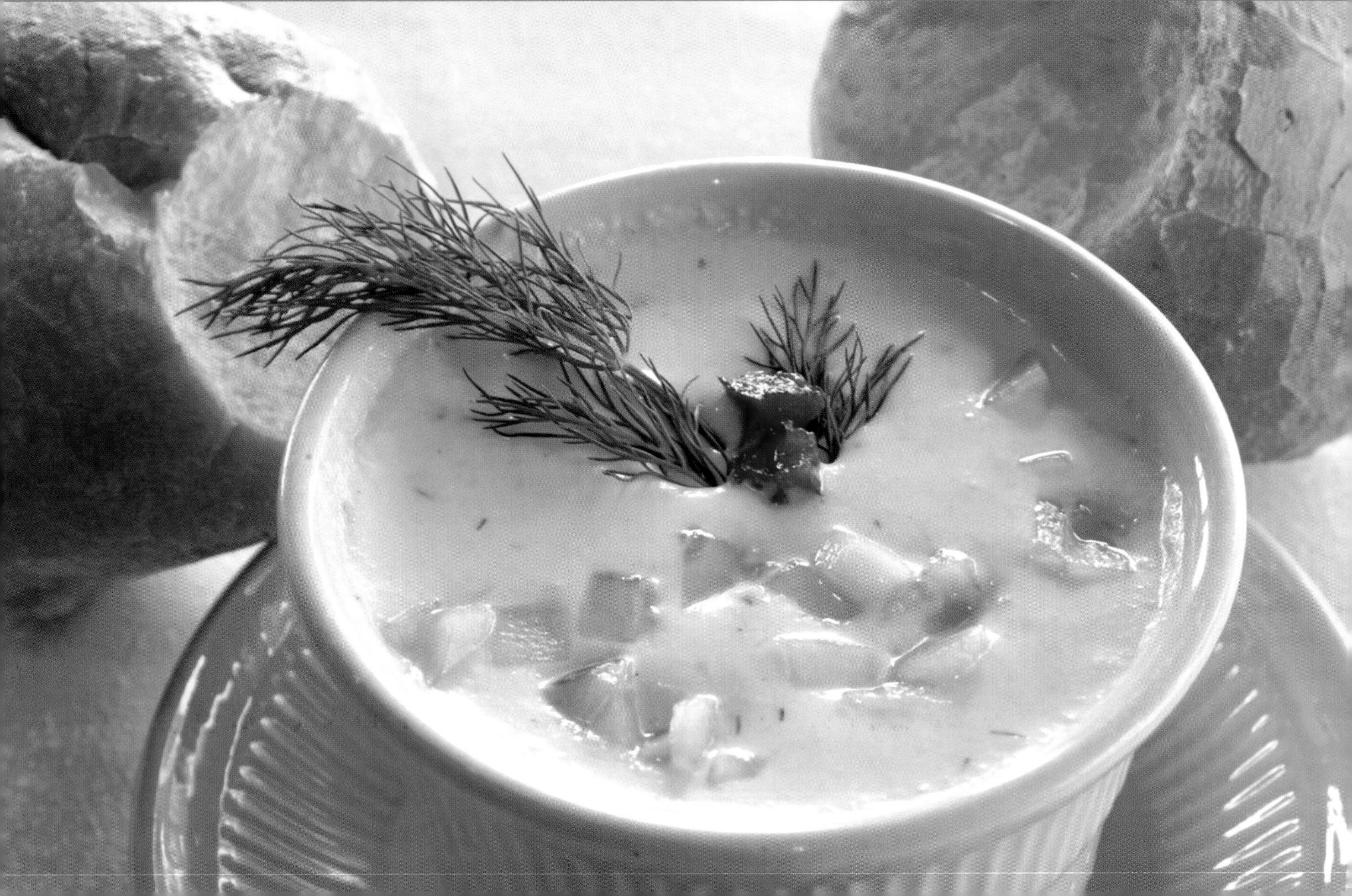

CHILLED CUCUMBER AND DILL SOUP

Yield: 6 servings (about 10 cups)

2 cups plain low-fat yogurt

1/2 cup sour cream

1/2 teaspoon Dijon mustard

1 teaspoon fresh lemon juice

3 cucumbers, peeled, seeded and coarsely chopped (about 7 cups), divided

1 small yellow onion, chopped

1 large dill pickle, chopped

2 cups heavy cream

1/4 cup finely chopped fresh dill

3/4 teaspoon salt or to taste

1/4 teaspoon ground white pepper or to taste

6 sprigs fresh dill, for garnish

In a food processor or large blender (see note), combine yogurt, sour cream, mustard and lemon juice. Set aside 1/2 cup cucumber for garnish; add remaining cucumber, onion and pickle to yogurt mixture, and process until vegetables are puréed completely. Add heavy cream; process just until smooth. Pour into a large bowl; stir in chopped dill, salt and pepper. Cover and chill for at least 2 hours. (For best flavor, chill overnight.)

Dice reserved cucumber into small pieces. Serve soup in chilled cups, garnished with diced cucumber and dill sprigs.

Note: If your blender or processor has less than a 12-cup capacity, process in batches. Be sure the vegetables are puréed completely before adding cream.

PER SERVING
calories 404 • fat 35g • % calories from fat 78 • saturated fat 21.5g • cholesterol 122mg • protein 7.5g • carbohydrate 15g • sugar 9g • fiber 1.5g • sodium 694mg • calcium 252mg • potassium 558mg

CORN CHOWDER

Yield: About 11 cups

7 tablespoons butter, divided

6 tablespoons all-purpose flour

5 slices bacon, diced

2 cups fresh corn kernels (see note)

1 medium onion, diced

1 medium carrot, minced

1 poblano pepper, seeded and diced

1½ teaspoons minced garlic

1 tablespoon ground cumin

1½ teaspoons chili powder

5 cups chicken stock

2 cups heavy cream

4 cups diced Yukon Gold potatoes

¼ teaspoon ground black pepper

Salt

To make a roux, melt 6 tablespoons butter over medium heat. Add flour; cook, stirring frequently, until very lightly browned, 3 to 5 minutes. Set aside.

In a large pot over medium heat, cook bacon in remaining 1 tablespoon butter until crisp, about 6 minutes. Add corn, onion, carrot and poblano pepper; sauté until vegetables begin to soften, about 5 minutes. Add garlic, cumin and chili powder; cook about 1 minute. Add stock. Bring to a boil, then reduce heat and simmer 10 minutes.

Add cream and potatoes; simmer until potatoes are tender, about 15 minutes. Gradually whisk in roux, cooking the soup for a few minutes after each addition, until soup reaches the desired consistency. (You may not need all of the roux.) Add black pepper and salt to taste.

Note: SqWires' chef said that fresh, seasonal corn tastes best, but frozen may be substituted.

PER 1-CUP SERVING

Calories 380 • fat 30g • % calories from fat 71 • saturated fat 17g • cholesterol 86mg • protein 5g • carbohydrate 23g • sugar 3g • fiber 3g • sodium 420mg • calcium 53mg • potassium 456mg

ROASTED BUTTERNUT SQUASH BISQUE WITH WILD RICE AND CRÈME ANISE

Yield: 6 servings (about 1 cup each)

FOR CRÈME ANISE:

1 cup heavy cream

5 tablespoons cultured buttermilk

1 tablespoon lemon juice

1 star anise

1 pinch salt

FOR WILD RICE:

2 tablespoons wild rice

1 cup vegetable stock

1 bay leaf

1 cinnamon stick

1 pinch salt

FOR BISQUE:

1 (2-pound) butternut squash

About 1 teaspoon Mixed-Spice Butter (see note)

3 tablespoons butter, divided

1 large white onion, diced

1 medium fennel bulb, white part only, diced

1 cinnamon stick

4 allspice berries

2 cloves

1 small bunch fresh thyme

4 cups vegetable stock or more if needed

Salt

Ground white pepper

To prepare Crème Anise: Stir together all ingredients in a small glass or plastic bowl. Mix well, cover tightly with plastic wrap and let sit overnight in a warm place (70 degrees). The next day, line a strainer with a coffee filter and place over a deep bowl. Spoon Crème Anise into the strainer. Let drain for several hours or until the consistency resembles sour cream. Remove star anise. Cover and refrigerate until needed, up to 1 week.

To prepare wild rice: Combine all ingredients in a small pot. Bring to a simmer, cover and cook until rice has split open, about 50 minutes. Drain; remove bay leaf and cinnamon stick. If making ahead, cover and refrigerate.

To prepare bisque: Preheat oven to 350 degrees. Split squash lengthwise and remove seeds; spread cut surfaces with Mixed-Spice Butter. Place squash, flesh side down, in a small roasting pan. Cover with foil and pierce small holes for steam to escape. Roast until tender, about 40 minutes; let cool to room temperature. Reserve pan juices. Remove skin from squash and discard; coarsely chop flesh and add to pan juices.

Place a large pot over medium heat; melt 2 tablespoons butter. Set the remaining 1 tablespoon butter aside to soften.

Add onion and fennel to the pot; cook, stirring occasionally, until tender and translucent, about 7 minutes. Add squash and pan juices; cook 2 minutes.

Meanwhile, combine cinnamon stick, allspice berries, cloves and thyme in a coffee filter; tie closed with kitchen string. Add spices and stock to the pot; bring to a simmer. Cook 20 minutes. Add wild rice; cook 5 minutes. Discard spices.

Purée soup with a hand-held electric mixer or in batches in a blender. Texture should be very smooth, with just the smallest bits of rice. Add stock if needed to thin the soup. Season with salt and white pepper. For best flavor, cover and refrigerate overnight.

Reheat just before serving and whisk in softened butter. Ladle into bowls; garnish each serving with a dollop of Crème Anise.

Note: To make Mixed-Spice Butter, beat together ¼ cup softened unsalted butter, a pinch each of salt and ground white pepper, and ground cinnamon, cloves, nutmeg, mace and allspice to taste.

PER SERVING
Calories 168 • fat 8g • % calories from fat 43 • saturated fat 5g • cholesterol 20mg • protein 2.5g • carbohydrate 21.5g • sugar 4g • fiber 3.5g • sodium 268mg • calcium 80mg • potassium 538mg

45

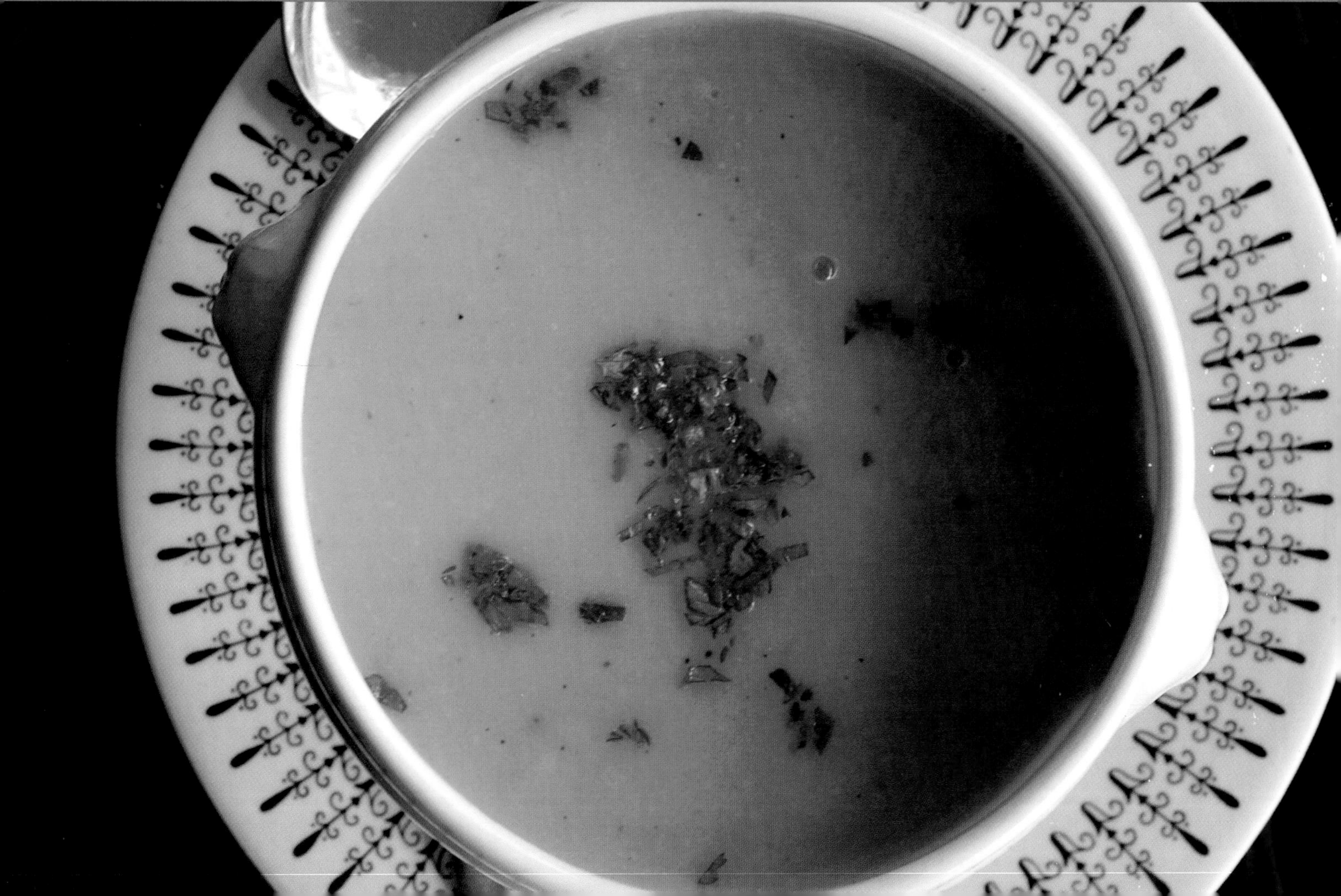

KABOCHA PUMPKIN SOUP

Yield: About 6 (1¼-cup) servings

½ cup olive oil

6 tablespoons (¾ stick) unsalted butter, divided

2 cups chopped yellow onion

2 to 3 teaspoons kosher salt

1 teaspoon freshly ground black pepper

1 pinch ground red (cayenne) pepper

5 allspice berries, crushed, or about ½ teaspoon ground allspice

1 cup dry white wine

1 large Golden Delicious apple, peeled, cored and chopped (about 2 cups)

1 (about 1½-pound) kabocha pumpkin, seeded, peeled and coarsely chopped (see note)

2 teaspoons lemon juice

Minced chives or parsley, for garnish

Combine oil, 2 tablespoons butter, onion, salt, black pepper, cayenne and allspice in a 5-quart or larger pot. Cook over medium heat until onion softens, but do not let it brown. Add wine; turn the heat to high, and cook until half of the wine has evaporated, about 4 minutes.

Add apple, then pumpkin; add enough water to cover (3 to 4 cups). Reduce heat; simmer until pumpkin is soft, about 20 minutes. Stir in lemon juice and remaining 4 tablespoons butter.

Transfer soup to a blender in batches; purée until smooth. (Fill the blender only halfway when working with hot liquids; pulse a few times to get started.) Taste and adjust seasonings. Serve immediately, garnished with chives or parsley.

Note: Kabocha (kah-BOH-chah) pumpkin is used in Japanese dishes and is often available at Asian markets. The pumpkins, harvested in the fall, become smaller and more difficult to find as the season passes; you might need two to yield enough pulp for this recipe. The slightly nutty-tasting kabocha must be peeled with a knife, as the rind is too thick for a vegetable peeler.

PER SERVING
calories 357 • fat 30.5g • % calories from fat 77 • saturated fat 10g • cholesterol 31mg • protein 1.5g • carbohydrate 17g • sugar 10.5g • fiber 3g • sodium 631mg • calcium 38mg • potassium 147mg

ROASTED RED PEPPER BISQUE

Yield: 8 servings (about 3/4 cup each)

Vegetable oil

5 large red bell peppers (see note)

4 cups chicken stock

1 1/2 teaspoons freshly grated nutmeg

2 bay leaves

1 tablespoon minced garlic

4 cups heavy cream

Kosher salt

Ground white pepper

6 tablespoons (3/4 stick) butter, melted

1/4 cup all-purpose flour

Preheat oven to 350 degrees. Lightly oil peppers; roast until the skins are brown, about 1 hour. Place peppers in a bowl; cover tightly. Let sit about 10 minutes, then peel and seed the peppers.

Combine roasted peppers, stock, nutmeg, bay leaves and garlic in a heavy pot; bring to a simmer. Cook for 1 hour.

Remove and discard the bay leaves. Purée the mixture with an immersible blender or in small batches in a food processor or blender. Pour through a fine-mesh strainer, discarding the solids. Return the soup to the pot. Add cream. Bring to a simmer; add salt and pepper to taste.

Melt butter in a small skillet. Stir in the flour until smooth, making a roux. Stir roux into the soup and simmer, stirring, until the soup reaches the desired consistency.

Note: Instead of roasting fresh peppers, you can substitute 2 (13 1/2-ounce) cans of roasted red peppers, drained. Monarch's chef recommended the Roland brand.

PER SERVING

calories 575 • fat 56g • % calories from fat 88 • saturated fat 33.5g • cholesterol 187mg • protein 4.5g • carbohydrate 14.5g • sugar 6.5g • fiber 2.5g • sodium 392mg • calcium 95mg • potassium 283mg   49

MARY BRENDAN'S TEA SHOP AT KERRY COTTAGE 2119 South Big Bend Boulevard • Maplewood, Mo. • 314-644-6279

WICKLOW SALAD

Yield: 4 servings

**Poppy Seed Dressing
(see recipe)**

**About 12 ounces torn mixed
greens, such as romaine
and spinach**

**1/2 cup finely shredded
Swiss cheese**

1/4 cup cashew halves

**6 tablespoons sweetened
dried cranberries**

**1 large unpeeled Gala apple,
cored and diced**

**1 large unpeeled Bosc pear,
cored and diced**

Toss dressing to taste with mixed greens; arrange on 4 chilled salad plates. Top each salad with cheese, cashews, cranberries, apple and pear, dividing evenly.

POPPY SEED DRESSING

Yield: 1 1/4 cups

1/2 cup granulated sugar

1/3 cup lemon juice

2 teaspoons finely chopped onion

1 teaspoon Irish whiskey mustard

1/2 teaspoon salt

2/3 cup vegetable oil

1 tablespoon poppy seeds

Mix sugar, lemon juice, onion, mustard and salt in a blender. With motor running, add oil in a slow, steady stream; process until thickened. Add poppy seeds; process a few seconds just to mix.

SALAD PER SERVING (WITHOUT DRESSING)
calories 219 • fat 8.5g • % calories from fat 35 • saturated fat 3g • cholesterol 13mg • protein 6.5g • carbohydrate 29g • sugar 18g • fiber 5g • sodium 54mg • calcium 184mg • potassium 431mg

DRESSING PER TABLESPOON
calories 90 • fat 7.5g • % calories from fat 75 • saturated fat 1g • cholesterol 0 • protein 0 • carbohydrate 5.5g • sugar 5g • fiber 0 • sodium 62mg • calcium 6mg • potassium 9mg

MAYFAIR SALAD DRESSING

Yield: About 1 pint

¾ cup corn oil

½ tablespoon ground black pepper

2 tablespoons plus 2 teaspoons prepared yellow mustard

1 rib celery, chopped

1 egg

½ medium yellow onion, chopped

¼ teaspoon granulated sugar

4 anchovy fillets

¼ cup mayonnaise

¼ teaspoon fresh minced garlic

Combine all ingredients in blender. Process until well mixed. Chill in refrigerator before serving. Refrigerate leftovers; use within a few days.

Note: This recipe uses an uncooked egg, which may be contaminated with salmonella. To avoid the potential of food poisoning, you can use Davidson's-brand eggs, which are pasteurized in the shell.

PER TABLESPOON
calories 63 • fat 6.5g • % calories from fat 93 • saturated fat 1g • cholesterol 8mg • protein 0.5g • carbohydrate 0.5g • sugar 0 • fiber 0 • sodium 46mg • calcium 4mg • potassium 15mg

MAIN DISHES

Potato 'n' Egg Bake • French Toast • Artichoke Parmesan Quiche • Baked Potato Soup • Lobster Bisque • Zuppa per le Feste (Holiday Soup) • Spicy Sherry-Onion Soup • Tortilla Soup • White Chili • Chickburger • Barbecued Chicken Pizza • Chicken Valle Douge • Pollo Agro Dolce (Venetian Sweet-and-Sour Chicken) • Involtini di Petti de Pollo (Chicken Spiedini) • Sesame Chicken • Red Curry Chicken Salad • Chicken Salad • Salade Niçoise • Salmon Fritters with Lemon-Caper Sauce • Grilled Mahi-Mahi with Lemon and Basil Aioli

Parmesan-Crusted Sole • Trout Meunière • Shellfish Sausage • Crawfish Cakes with Cajun Aioli • Sautéed Scallops with Chardonnay Sauce • Shrimp Sara • Bobo de Camarao Yemanja • Grinders • Jambalaya • Steak Salad • Tenderloin Spiedini • Filet Zanti • Mushroom Cheese Steak • Low-Country Meat Pies • Veal Saltimbocca • Liver Sweet and Sour • Grilled Prairie Grass Farms Lamb Chops in Asian Apricot Glaze • Pork Tenderloin with Cranberry Ginger Chutney • Pork Tenderloin with Raspberry Sauce • Chile Verde • BLT Pasta • Morel Mushroom Pasta • Rigatoni with Eggplant • Linguine with Clams • Penne Borghese • Pasta con Broccoli • Thai Red Curry Dragonfly Pasta • Szechwan Eggplant • Green Bean and Mushroom Stir-Fry (Dau Que Xao Nam)

COMPANION BAKEHOUSE AND CAFÉ   8143 Maryland Avenue   •   Clayton, Mo.   •   314-721-5454   •   www.companionbaking.com/cafe

POTATO 'N' EGG BAKE

Yield: 6 servings

3 tablespoons butter, plus more to prepare pan

2/3 cup all-purpose flour

1 cup whole milk

1 1/4 cups heavy cream

2 1/4 ounces grated Gruyère cheese (about 1 cup)

1 tablespoon plus 1 teaspoon grainy Dijon mustard

1 1/8 teaspoons salt

1/4 teaspoon ground red (cayenne) pepper

1/8 teaspoon ground white pepper

7 large eggs

1 baked potato, cooled, peeled and cut into bite-size chunks, optional

Toppings of your choice, such as 6 slices cooked bacon (see tester's note)

4 ounces shredded cheese, such as Cheddar (see tester's note)

Preheat oven to 350 degrees. Butter a 7-by-10-inch baking dish that is at least 2 inches deep.

In a skillet over medium-high heat, melt butter; whisk in flour and cook just until flour is golden. Whisk in milk and cream. Cook until mixture is as thick as a milkshake, about 8 minutes, whisking constantly. Whisk in grated Gruyère, mustard, salt, cayenne and white pepper. Remove from heat.

Break eggs into a large bowl; whisk until well blended. Gradually whisk milk mixture into eggs.

Pour egg mixture into baking dish; add potato chunks. Bake 30 minutes. Reduce oven temperature to 325 degrees. Arrange toppings and shredded cheese over egg mixture; bake 15 minutes or until cheese has melted and edges of casserole begin to brown. Let cool 5 minutes before serving.

Tester's note: We used ham with shredded Italian four-cheese blend in one test and crabmeat with shredded Cheddar in another.

PER SERVING
calories 581 • fat 47g • % calories from fat 73 • saturated fat 26g • cholesterol 419mg • protein 24.5g • carbohydrate 15g • sugar 3g • fiber 0.5g • sodium 959mg • calcium 442mg • potassium 275mg

FRENCH TOAST

Yield: 6 servings

6 eggs

2 cups milk

1/8 teaspoon ground cinnamon

12 slices day-old raisin bread (about 1/2 inch thick)

Nonstick cooking spray

Powdered sugar

Warm Fruit Compote (see recipe)

Beat eggs with milk and cinnamon. Dip bread in egg mixture, but do not allow to soak.

Spray a griddle with nonstick spray; grill bread until golden brown on both sides. Cut bread on the diagonal to form triangles, dust with powdered sugar and serve immediately with Warm Fruit Compote.

WARM FRUIT COMPOTE

Yield: 6 servings

1/4 cup freshly squeezed orange juice

1/4 cup plus 2 tablespoons honey

1 1/2 cups orange sections (about 3 large navel oranges)

1 1/2 cups fresh strawberries

1 1/2 cups fresh raspberries

4 kiwi, sliced (about 1 1/2 cups)

1 1/2 cups chopped fresh pineapple

1 mango, chopped (about 1 cup)

In a large saucepan, bring orange juice and honey to a boil. Let boil 30 seconds. Remove from heat; stir in orange sections, strawberries, raspberries, kiwi, pineapple and mango. Keep warm until serving.

FRENCH TOAST PER SERVING
Calories 272 • fat 9g • % calories from fat 30 • cholesterol 222mg • protein 13g • carbohydrate 37g • fiber 2g • sodium 293mg • calcium 171mg

COMPOTE PER SERVING
Calories 188 • fat 1g • % calories from fat 5 • cholesterol 0 • protein 2g • carbohydrate 48g • fiber 6.5g • sodium 2mg • calcium 58mg

ARTICHOKE PARMESAN QUICHE

Yield: 6 servings

**Pastry for single-crust
9-inch pie**

**½ cup grated Parmesan
cheese, plus additional for
garnish**

**1 (14-ounce) can artichoke
hearts, drained**

**1¼ cups chopped or
shredded Swiss cheese**

**3 ounces cream cheese,
softened**

½ teaspoon ground nutmeg

⅛ teaspoon salt

**1 cup plus 2 tablespoons
evaporated milk**

3 eggs

Preheat oven to 450 degrees. Line a 9-inch deep-dish pie plate with pastry; prick bottom and sides several times with a fork. Bake 7 to 8 minutes, until beginning to brown. Decrease oven temperature to 400 degrees.

Sprinkle ½ cup Parmesan evenly over crust. Squeeze liquid from artichoke hearts, blot dry and chop well; distribute over Parmesan. Sprinkle Swiss cheese over artichokes.

In small bowl of electric mixer, beat cream cheese with nutmeg and salt until light. Gradually beat in milk, then eggs, one at a time; continue beating until mixture is frothy. Pour into crust.

Bake about 40 minutes or until light golden brown. Before serving, sprinkle each slice liberally with additional Parmesan.

PER SERVING
calories 396 • fat 26g • % calories from fat 59 • saturated fat 13.5g • cholesterol 162mg • protein 19g • carbohydrate 21.5g • sugar 9g • fiber 3g • sodium 623mg • calcium 405mg • potassium 243mg

BAKED POTATO SOUP

Yield: 7 servings (about 1 1/2 cups each)

8 large russet potatoes, scrubbed well

3 tablespoons butter

2 large onions, finely chopped

2 tablespoons chopped parsley

1 tablespoon Italian seasoning mix

1/2 teaspoon salt or to taste

1/4 teaspoon ground pepper or to taste

3 cups chicken stock

3 cups half-and-half or whole milk

1/2 cup sour cream

1 cup shredded Cheddar cheese

1/2 cup crumbled cooked bacon

1/3 cup chopped green onions or chives

Preheat oven to 350 degrees; bake potatoes about 45 minutes or until tender. Let cool, peel and cut into 1/3-inch cubes.

In a heavy soup kettle, melt butter over medium heat; cook onions until translucent. Add parsley, Italian seasoning, salt and pepper. Add chicken stock and potatoes. Bring to a boil over medium-high heat; reduce heat and simmer gently for 15 minutes, stirring occasionally.

Stir in half-and-half or milk. Return to a boil, then reduce heat and simmer 15 minutes, stirring often to prevent sticking. Add sour cream; simmer 5 minutes.

Ladle into soup bowls; top with Cheddar, bacon and green onions or chives.

PER SERVING
calories 499 • fat 28.5g • % calories from fat 51 • saturated fat 17g • cholesterol 96mg • protein 15g • carbohydrate 48g • sugar 10g • fiber 4g • sodium 740mg • calcium 274mg • potassium 1,037mg

LOBSTER BISQUE

Yield: 6 cups

6 cups water

1 (8-ounce) frozen lobster tail (in shell)

½ cup (1 stick) plus 2 tablespoons butter, divided

1 medium onion, chopped

¼ teaspoon minced fresh garlic

¼ cup diced celery

2 bay leaves

2 cups heavy cream

¼ teaspoon salt or to taste

1 dash ground red (cayenne) pepper

1 dash ground white pepper

1½ tablespoons lobster base (see note)

1 cup all-purpose flour

6 tablespoons cream sherry

Bring water to a boil in a stockpot; add lobster tail and boil 20 minutes.

Meanwhile, melt 2 tablespoons butter in a medium skillet. Add onion, garlic, celery and bay leaves; sauté until vegetables soften. Set aside.

Remove cooked lobster tail; set aside to cool. Add cream and sautéed vegetables to stockpot; bring to a boil, then cook 10 minutes. Stir in salt, cayenne, white pepper and lobster base.

In a small skillet, melt remaining ½ cup butter; whisk in flour to make a roux. Add enough roux to the simmering soup mixture to achieve the desired thickness. Simmer 20 minutes.

Strain soup through a colander into a second pot. Remove lobster tail from shell; chop meat into small chunks. Stir lobster and sherry into bisque; simmer 5 minutes. Serve hot.

Note: Lobster base is a highly concentrated, pastelike soup base. It is available from gourmet stores and some spice shops. Seafood base may be substituted.

PER 1-CUP SERVING
calories 582 • fat 50g • % calories from fat 77 • saturated fat 31g • cholesterol 190mg • protein 12g • carbohydrate 19.5g • sugar 3g • fiber 0.5g • sodium 821mg • calcium 87mg • potassium 235mg

DOMINIC'S ON THE HILL 5101 Wilson Avenue • St. Louis • 314-771-1632
DOMINIC'S TRATTORIA 200 South Brentwood Boulevard • Clayton, Mo. • 314-863-4567 • www.dominicsrestaurant.com

ZUPPA PER LE FESTE (HOLIDAY SOUP)

Yield: 10 cups (about 6 servings)

FOR MEATBALLS:

7 ounces lean ground beef

1 egg

¼ cup dry bread crumbs

¼ cup grated Parmesan cheese

¼ teaspoon salt

⅛ teaspoon ground black pepper

FOR SOUP:

3 tablespoons olive oil

1 small onion, chopped

1 small carrot, diced

1 tomato, peeled and chopped

2 cloves garlic, finely chopped

2 ounces fresh spinach, chopped (about 1½ cups)

7 cups chicken or beef broth, heated

2 cups cooked rice

3 tablespoons fresh parsley, chopped

Salt, optional

Ground black pepper, optional

Parmesan cheese, for garnish

To prepare meatballs: Preheat oven to 400 degrees. In a bowl, mix together beef, egg, bread crumbs, cheese, salt and pepper. Form ¾-inch meatballs. Place on a parchment-lined baking sheet; bake until nicely browned, about 10 minutes. Set aside.

To prepare soup: Heat oil over medium heat in a large saucepan or Dutch oven. Stir in onion; cook 5 minutes. Add carrot, tomato, garlic and spinach; cook over medium heat, stirring often, about 5 minutes.

Pour in hot broth; stir well and bring to a boil. Add meatballs; simmer 2 minutes. Stir in rice; sprinkle with parsley. Add salt and pepper to taste. Allow soup to stand for a few minutes, then serve with grated Parmesan on the side.

PER SERVING
calories 286 • fat 14g • % calories from fat 44 • saturated fat 3.5g • cholesterol 54mg • protein 17.5g • carbohydrate 22.5g • sugar 3g • fiber 1g • sodium 1,154mg • calcium 98mg • potassium 537mg

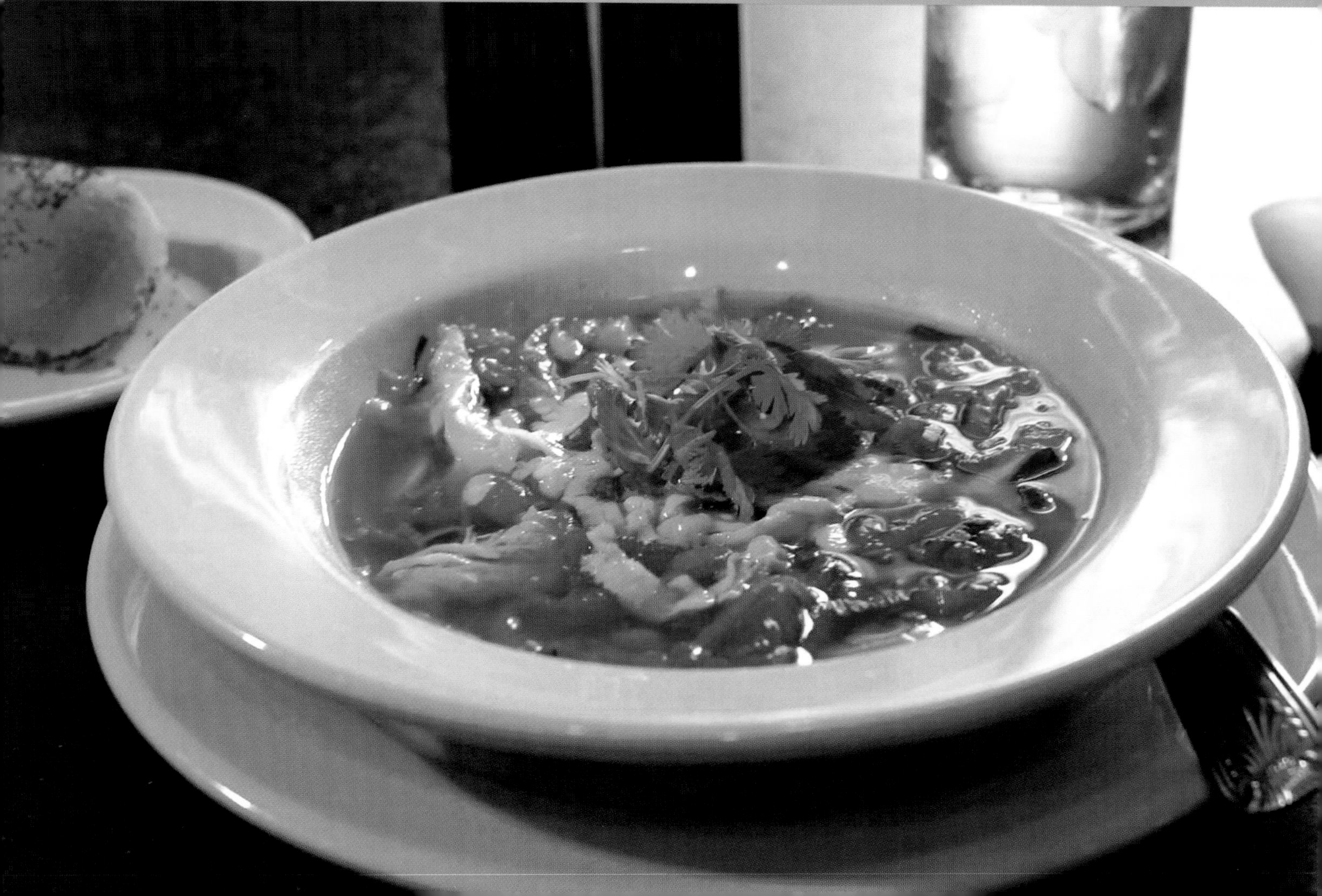

SPICY SHERRY-ONION SOUP

Yield: 6 servings

2 tablespoons olive oil

¼ cup sliced leeks, rinsed well

¼ cup sliced garlic

2 cups sliced onions, divided

Salt

½ teaspoon red pepper flakes

1 tablespoon chopped fresh cilantro

½ cup dry sherry

3 cups chicken stock (see note)

1 to 2 tablespoons fish sauce (see note)

Ground black pepper

**1 cup chopped Roma tomatoes or
    1 (14.5-ounce) can diced tomatoes,
    undrained (see note)**

8 ounces smoked chicken, shredded

1 cup diced mozzarella

Lime wedges, for garnish

Cilantro sprigs, for garnish

Heat oil in a 3-quart pan over medium heat. Add leeks, garlic and 1 cup onions; sauté until sizzling. Add a pinch of salt, reduce heat to medium-low, and cook until onions are tender and slightly browned, 8 to 10 minutes.

Add pepper flakes, cilantro, sherry, chicken stock and remaining 1 cup onions. Bring soup to a boil, then reduce heat and cook about 4 minutes. Stir in fish sauce, salt and pepper to taste and tomatoes; cook until tomatoes begin to soften, about 2 minutes.

Ladle into serving bowls; divide chicken and cheese evenly among bowls. Garnish with lime wedges and cilantro sprigs.

Notes: If using canned chicken broth, omit additional salt. Fish sauce is a salty, uniquely flavored liquid sold in many supermarkets and in Asian markets. Using canned tomatoes rather than fresh gives the soup a more "tomato-y" aspect.

PER SERVING
calories 240 • fat 12g • % calories from fat 45 • saturated fat 4g • cholesterol 46mg • protein 19g • carbohydrate 11.5g • sugar 6g • fiber 2g • sodium 734mg • calcium 199mg

OZZIE'S RESTAURANT AND SPORTS BAR 645 West Port Plaza • Maryland Heights, Mo. • 314-434-1000 • www.ozziesrestaurantandsportsbar.com

TORTILLA SOUP

Yield: 6 servings (about 1 1/2 cups each)

1 (6-inch) corn tortilla

Vegetable oil, for frying

2 1/2 tablespoons chicken base (concentrated broth sold near canned soups)

2 tablespoons lemon juice

3/4 teaspoon dried oregano

3/4 teaspoon dried basil

1 teaspoon chipotle paste or to taste (see note)

1 1/2 teaspoons ground white pepper

2 bay leaves

1 1/4 cups tomato sauce

2 tablespoons cornstarch

1 medium tomato, peeled and cut into thin strips (about 1 cup)

2 chicken breast halves, cooked and cut into 1-inch cubes, divided

3 tablespoons chopped cilantro, divided

1 1/2 cups grated Monterey Jack cheese, divided

Cut tortilla into thin strips. Pour about 1/2 inch of oil into a small skillet; place over medium-high heat. When hot, add tortilla strips in batches, frying until crispy. Drain well on paper towels; set aside to use as a garnish.

In a large pan, combine 6 cups water and chicken base; stir until dissolved. Stir in lemon juice, oregano, basil, chipotle paste, white pepper, bay leaves and tomato sauce. Bring to a boil, then reduce heat to medium and simmer 15 minutes. Dissolve cornstarch in 3 tablespoons water; stir into simmering liquid. Return to a boil, stirring often. Remove bay leaves.

Divide tomato strips and chicken among soup bowls; ladle in soup. Top each serving with 1/2 tablespoon cilantro, 1/4 cup cheese and a sprinkling of tortilla strips.

Note: To make chipotle paste, buy a can of chipotle peppers in adobo sauce from the Mexican food aisle. Empty the can into a blender or food processor, and process until the mixture is puréed. To store, spread on a parchment-lined pan and freeze; place frozen paste in an airtight bag. Break off pieces as needed for seasoning.

PER SERVING

Calories 236 • fat 12.5g • % calories from fat 48 • saturated fat 6g • cholesterol 53mg • protein 18g • carbohydrate 13g • sugar 4g • fiber 1.5g • sodium 1,833mg • calcium 226mg • potassium 315mg

THE BLUE OWL RESTAURANT AND BAKERY Second and Mill streets • Kimmswick, Mo. • 636-464-3128 • www.theblueowl.com

WHITE CHILI

Yield: 12 (about 1-cup) servings

4½ to 5 pounds boneless skin-on chicken breasts

1 tablespoon olive oil

2 medium onions, chopped

4 cloves garlic, minced

2 (4-ounce) cans chopped mild green chiles, undrained

2 teaspoons ground cumin

1½ teaspoons dried oregano, crumbled

¼ teaspoon ground red (cayenne) pepper

3 (15- to 16-ounce) cans Great Northern beans, undrained

6 cups chicken stock or canned broth

3 cups (12 ounces) grated Monterey Jack cheese, plus more for optional garnish

Salt

Ground black pepper

Sour cream, for optional garnish

Place chicken in a large, heavy saucepan. Add cold water to cover; bring to a simmer. Cook until just tender, about 15 minutes. Drain and let cool. Remove skin. Cut chicken into cubes.

Add oil to the same pot; place over medium-high heat. When oil is hot, add onions; sauté until translucent, about 10 minutes. Stir in garlic, then chiles, cumin, oregano and cayenne; sauté 2 minutes.

Add beans and their liquid and stock; bring to a boil. Reduce heat; add chicken and cheese. Stir until cheese melts. Season to taste with salt and pepper. Ladle chili into bowls. Garnish with sour cream or cheese.

CHICKBURGER

Yield: 5 servings

1 pound finely chopped cooked chicken or turkey (white or dark meat)

2 tablespoons barbecue seasoning or to taste

5 tablespoons granulated sugar

1 tablespoon celery salt

3/4 teaspoon ground black pepper

10 to 12 ounces chicken broth

5 toasted hamburger buns

Tartar sauce

Lettuce leaves

Sliced tomato

Preheat oven to 350 degrees. Toss chicken with barbecue seasoning, sugar, celery salt and pepper; transfer to a 9-by-13-inch pan. Cover mixture with chicken broth. Bake, uncovered, for 35 to 40 minutes or until a crust forms on top.

Mixture should be moist when it's removed from the oven. If it's too dry, add a little more chicken broth.

Serve chicken on toasted buns with tartar sauce, lettuce and tomato.

PER SERVING
calories 317 • fat 5g • % calories from fat 14 • saturated fat 1.5g • cholesterol 79mg • protein 33g • carbohydrate 35g • sugar 16g • fiber 1g • sodium 1,897mg • calcium 90mg • potassium 280mg

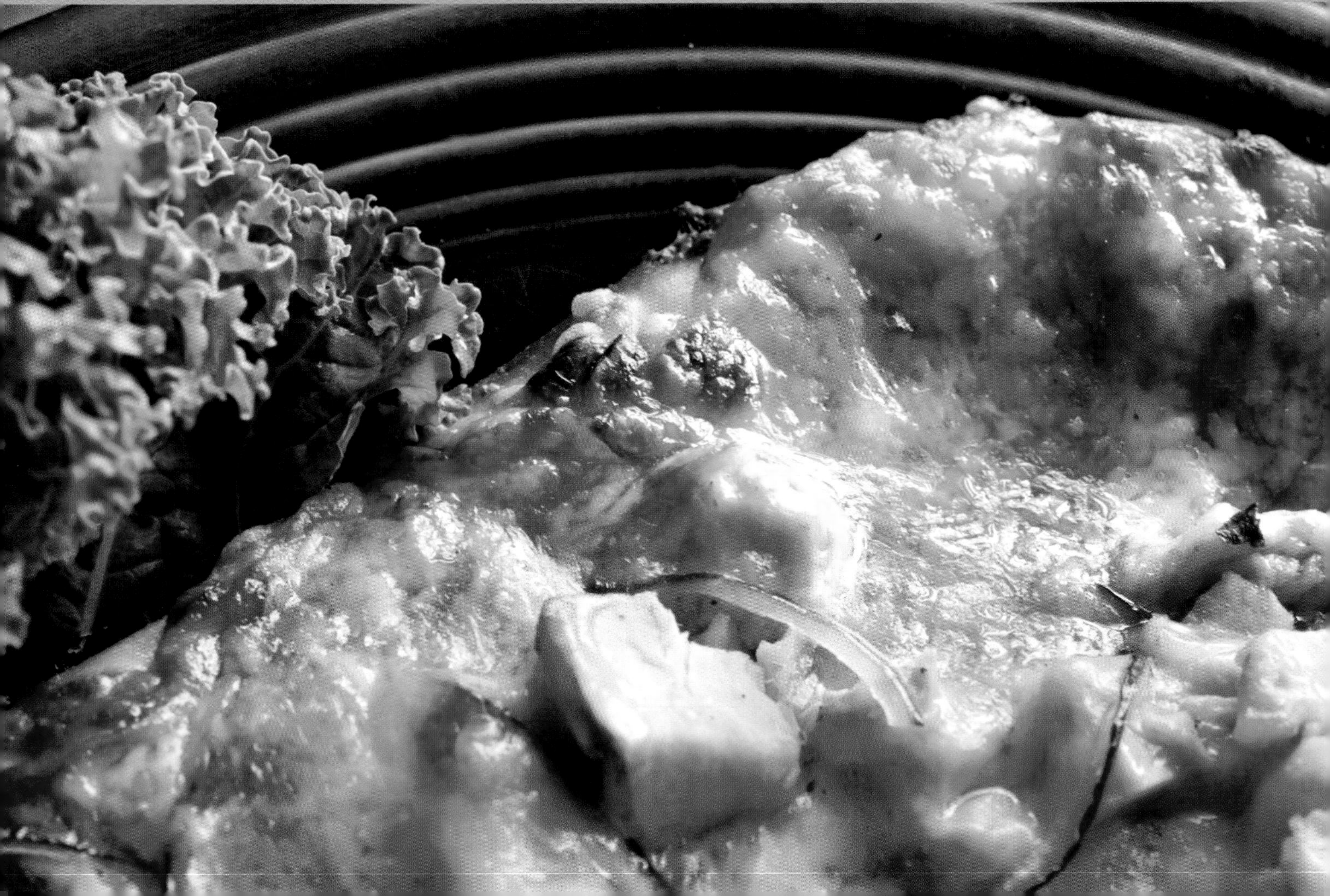

BARBECUED CHICKEN PIZZA

Yield: 1 (10-inch) pizza; 2 servings

1½ teaspoons sweet-flavored dry rib rub, such as Williams brand

6 ounces skinless, boneless chicken breast

1 tablespoon honey

½ cup barbecue sauce, such as Blues Hog brand

6 ounces refrigerated or handmade pizza dough (see recipe)

½ cup shredded Cheddar cheese

½ cup shredded Jack cheese

½ cup shredded Swiss cheese

2 tablespoons thinly sliced red onion

Sprinkle rub on chicken; smoke over hickory until the internal temperature reaches 165 degrees. Let cool, then cut chicken into ½-inch pieces.

Place a baking stone in the oven; preheat the oven to 425 degrees. Stir honey into barbecue sauce; set aside.

Roll pizza dough thin, into about a rough 10-inch circle; bake on the hot stone 3 minutes. Remove from the oven; spread sauce over the crust. Top with chicken, then cheeses and onion. Return to the oven; bake until crust is browned, 9 to 11 minutes.

PIZZA DOUGH

Yield: About 12 ounces; enough for 2 crusts

½ teaspoon granulated sugar

¼ cup water (105 to 115 degrees)

1⅛ teaspoons active dry yeast (½ package)

1 teaspoon salt

1¾ cups all-purpose flour, divided

2 tablespoons olive oil

¼ cup milk, at room temperature

Stir sugar into warm water; stir in yeast and let stand until foamy, about 3 minutes.

In the work bowl of a food processor fitted with the steel knife or dough blade, combine salt and 1½ cups flour. Add yeast mixture, oil and milk. Pulse to combine; dough should begin to form in a few seconds. Add a spoonful of the remaining flour; pulse to incorporate, then continue adding flour and pulsing just until dough forms a ball and cleans the sides of the bowl.

Note: Jack and Mary Billings developed this easy recipe, which closely resembles Trailhead's crust. It makes enough dough for two Barbecued Chicken Pizzas, or freeze half for future use.

PER SERVING
calories 734 • fat 35g • % calories from fat 43 • saturated fat 18g • cholesterol 131mg • protein 48.5g • carbohydrate 58g • sugar 19g • fiber 2.5g • sodium 2,300mg • calcium 722mg • potassium 516mg

CRUST PER SERVING (based on 4 servings)
calories 269 • fat 8g • % calories from fat 27 • saturated fat 1.5g • cholesterol 2mg • protein 6.5g • carbohydrate 43.5g • sugar 2g • fiber 2g • sodium 596mg • calcium 28mg • potassium 104mg

CHICKEN VALLE DOUGE

Yield: 1 serving

1 (8-ounce) whole skinless, boneless chicken breast (see note)

Salt

Ground white pepper

2 tablespoons clarified butter (see note)

¾ cup sliced button mushrooms

2 teaspoons granulated sugar

½ Red Delicious apple, peeled, cored and sliced about ½ inch thick

2 tablespoons apple brandy (applejack or Calvados), warmed slightly

½ cup heavy cream

1 to 2 tablespoons chicken stock, optional

Season chicken to taste with salt and white pepper. Place a medium skillet over medium-high heat. Add clarified butter to skillet, then add seasoned chicken. Sauté until light brown, about 2 minutes. Turn chicken; immediately add mushrooms, sugar and apple slices. Cook about 2 minutes, stirring mushrooms and apples, until chicken is browned on second side.

Remove skillet from burner; add brandy. Touch a lighted match to the contents of the skillet to flame the brandy. When the flames subside, return to heat.

Add cream, reduce heat, and let the chicken finish cooking and the sauce thicken, about 6 to 8 minutes. (If the sauce becomes too thick, thin it with chicken stock.)

Place chicken on serving plate; pour sauce over chicken.

Note: Most boneless, skinless chicken breasts sold in grocery stores are larger breast halves (about 8 ounces each). To use a large breast half, butterfly it by cutting into the thickest, long side about three-fourths of the way through and opening the meat like a book.

To make clarified butter, melt about 4 tablespoons unsalted butter in a small pan. Skim off and discard the foam. Pour off the golden melted butter, discarding the milky solids that collect at the bottom of the pan.

POLLO AGRO DOLCE (VENETIAN SWEET-AND-SOUR CHICKEN)

Yield: 4 servings

½ **teaspoon ground cloves**

1 **teaspoon finely grated orange zest (colored portion of peel)**

½ **cup plus 6 tablespoons balsamic vinegar, divided**

1 **teaspoon chopped fresh mint leaves**

¼ **cup plus 4 teaspoons olive oil, divided**

Salt

½ **teaspoon ground black pepper**

4 **(8-ounce) boneless, skinless chicken breasts**

4 **teaspoons unsalted butter**

1 **medium red onion, thinly sliced**

2 **medium red bell peppers, julienned (cut into matchstick-size pieces)**

6 **white button mushrooms, thinly sliced**

¼ **cup golden raisins**

¼ **cup dark raisins**

¼ **cup pine nuts**

¼ **cup sweet vermouth**

Chicken stock

Mix cloves, zest, ½ cup vinegar, mint, ¼ cup oil, ½ teaspoon salt and pepper in a bowl. Add chicken, toss to coat, and marinate in refrigerator 3 hours or overnight. Drain chicken, discarding marinade.

Place a skillet large enough to hold the chicken without crowding over medium-high heat. Add the remaining 4 teaspoons oil and butter. When the butter melts, add onion, bell peppers and mushrooms. Sauté about 4 minutes, until vegetables begin to brown. Use tongs or a slotted spoon to transfer vegetables to a bowl; keep warm.

Add chicken breasts to the skillet, with what was the skin-side down; sear lightly. Turn chicken, add raisins and pine nuts, and cook 1 to 2 minutes, until pine nuts begin to brown. Add the remaining 6 tablespoons balsamic vinegar and vermouth; bring to a simmer. Season lightly with salt, then reduce heat to medium.

Cook until chicken is just done and sauce is reduced to the consistency of a light syrup. If the sauce is overly reduced before the chicken is done, add small ladlefuls of chicken stock. If the sauce is too thin when the chicken is done, remove the chicken, then continue to cook the sauce to reduce further.

When sauce is the correct consistency, stir in vegetables. Taste; add salt if needed. Turn chicken pieces over to coat with sauce, then arrange chicken on serving plates or a platter. Spoon vegetables and sauce over chicken.

PER SERVING
calories 531 • fat 20g • % calories from fat 34 • saturated fat 5g • cholesterol 142mg • protein 57g • carbohydrate 31g • sugar 23g • fiber 3g • sodium 253mg • calcium 63mg • potassium 1,067mg

INVOLTINI DI PETTI DE POLLO (CHICKEN SPIEDINI)

Yield: 2 servings

FOR STUFFING:

- ½ cup diced pancetta (about 5 slices)
- ½ cup diced onion
- ½ cup chopped mushrooms
- ¼ cup extra-virgin olive oil
- ¼ cup white wine
- 1 cup chopped fresh spinach
- 1 cup dry Italian-seasoned bread crumbs
- ½ cup grated Parmesan
- ½ cup shredded mozzarella
- Salt
- Freshly ground black pepper

FOR CHICKEN:

- 4 large boneless, skinless chicken breast halves
- 2 tablespoons olive oil
- ½ cup Italian-seasoned dry bread crumbs

FOR SAUCE:

- ½ cup (1 stick) butter, softened, divided
- 1 cup sliced mushrooms
- ¼ cup white wine
- 1½ cups beef stock
- 1½ to 2 tablespoons lemon juice
- ¼ cup all-purpose flour
- Salt
- Freshly ground black pepper

To prepare stuffing: In a medium saucepan over medium-high heat, cook pancetta, onion and mushrooms in olive oil until lightly browned. Stir in wine, scraping up any browned bits. Add spinach, bread crumbs and cheeses; stir until thoroughly mixed. Add salt and pepper to taste. Set aside to cool.

To prepare chicken: Preheat the oven to 375 degrees. Rinse chicken and pat dry; pound to a uniform thickness of about ⅛ inch. Place one-fourth of the stuffing on each piece of chicken, and spread to cover; roll up tightly. Rub with olive oil and coat lightly with bread crumbs. Arrange on a baking sheet. Bake 25 to 30 minutes, until cooked through.

While chicken bakes, prepare sauce: In a medium saucepan, melt ¼ cup butter. Add mushrooms; sauté for 1 minute. Add wine; cook about 2 minutes to reduce. Add stock and lemon juice.

In a small dish, knead flour into remaining ¼ cup butter. Whisk butter-flour mixture into stock mixture. Cook, stirring occasionally, until sauce reaches desired consistency. Add salt and pepper to taste. (You should have about 2 cups of sauce.)

To serve, arrange chicken on plates; spoon sauce over the chicken.

PER SERVING
calories 1,869 • fat 107.5g • % calories from fat 52 • saturated fat 37.5g • cholesterol 416mg • protein 142g • carbohydrate 75g • sugar 6.5g • fiber 4.5g • sodium 3,243mg • calcium 787mg • potassium 997mg

SESAME CHICKEN

Yield: 3 servings

2 teaspoons sesame seeds

³/₄ pound skinless, boneless chicken breasts

¹/₂ egg white (about 1 tablespoon)

1 teaspoon cornstarch

2 to 3 tablespoons water

1 teaspoon vegetable oil, plus more for deep-frying

2 teaspoons chopped garlic

2 teaspoons chopped green onion

2 teaspoons soy sauce

2 tablespoons granulated sugar

¹/₂ teaspoon ground black pepper

Shredded cabbage

Steamed broccoli florets

Toast sesame seeds in a small dry skillet, stirring constantly. Transfer sesame seeds to a small bowl; set aside.

Slice chicken into strips ¹/₈ inch thick and about 1¹/₂ inches long. In a small bowl, whisk together egg white, cornstarch, water and 1 teaspoon vegetable oil; add chicken and stir well to coat.

In a wok or large nonstick skillet, heat 2 to 3 cups oil to 325 degrees. Add chicken; stir to make sure pieces don't stick together. Fry until cooked through, 1 to 2 minutes. Turn off burner and remove chicken with a slotted spoon; drain well.

Pour out the oil, leaving just enough to coat the pan. Place the pan over medium heat. Add garlic and green onion; stir-fry until fragrant. Stir in soy sauce, sugar, pepper and sesame seeds. When sugar is dissolved and mixture is well-combined, return chicken to the pan; stir until the chicken is evenly coated with sauce.

Place cabbage on a serving dish, top with chicken and surround with steamed broccoli.

PER SERVING
calories 232 • fat 8g • % calories from fat 31 • saturated fat 1.5g • cholesterol 66mg • protein 28g • carbohydrate 12g • sugar 8.5g • fiber 0.5g • sodium 377mg • calcium 20mg • potassium 308mg

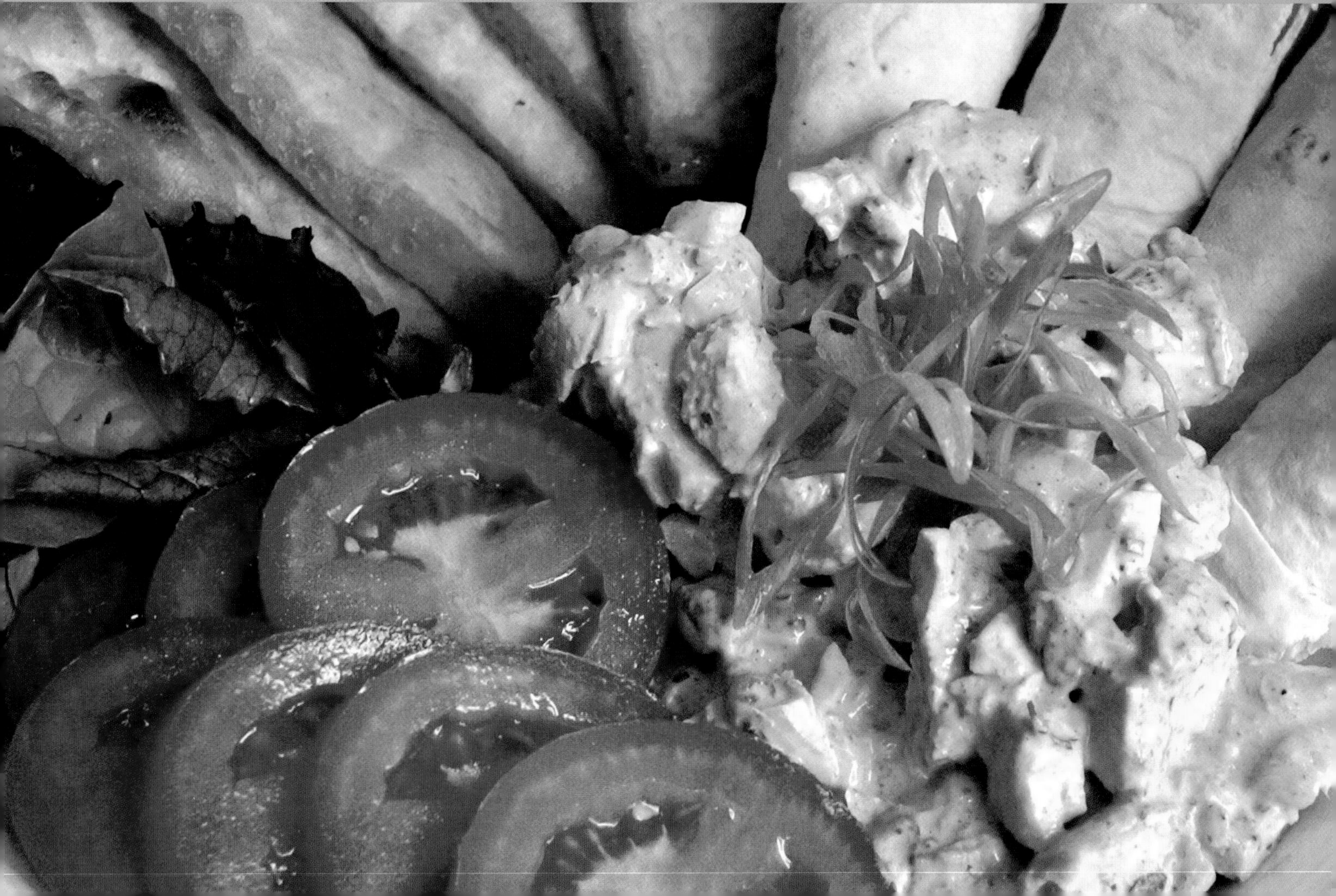

RED CURRY CHICKEN SALAD

Yield: 8 servings

1 cup mayonnaise

2 tablespoons vindaloo paste or more to taste (see note)

2 teaspoons minced garlic

3/4 teaspoon salt

1/4 teaspoon ground pepper

1/4 cup white wine

1/4 cup shelled pistachios

1/4 cup golden raisins

1/2 cup minced onion

1/2 cup diced celery

2 1/2 pounds baked boneless, skinless chicken breast, cut into 1/2-inch cubes

Fresh tomatoes, for garnish

Pita wedges, for garnish

In a large bowl, combine mayonnaise, vindaloo paste, garlic, salt, pepper and wine; whisk until thoroughly combined. With a rubber spatula, fold in pistachios, raisins, onion and celery. Gently fold in chicken; cover and chill.

Serve on chilled plates, garnished with sliced or chopped tomatoes and pita.

Note: Vindaloo paste is an Indian curry seasoning available at ethnic markets. Although it is not the hottest of curries, a larger amount can make this chicken salad quite spicy.

PER SERVING
calories 424 • fat 28g • % calories from fat 59 • saturated fat 5g • cholesterol 103mg • protein 34.5g • carbohydrate 8g • sugar 4.5g • fiber 1.5g • sodium 592mg • calcium 30mg • potassium 492mg

CHICKEN SALAD

Yield: About 5½ cups

1¾ **pounds boneless,**
skinless chicken breasts,
grilled

½ **cup slivered almonds,**
toasted

3 **green onions, sliced**

⅜ **cup green seedless**
grapes

⅜ **cup red seedless grapes**

6½ **tablespoons mayonnaise**

½ **cup sour cream**

3 **tablespoons plus**
1 teaspoon honey

Salt

Ground pepper

Cut chicken into ½-inch cubes. Place in a large bowl. Add almonds, onions and grapes; toss to mix. In a separate bowl, whisk together mayonnaise, sour cream, honey, and salt and pepper to taste. Pour over chicken mixture; toss to coat thoroughly.

PER ½-CUP SERVING
calories 215 • fat 12g • % calories from fat 50 • saturated fat 3g • cholesterol 52mg • protein 18g • carbohydrate 9g • sugar 7g • fiber 1g • sodium 98mg • calcium 37mg • potassium 270mg

SALADE NIÇOISE

Yield: 1 serving

2 small red potatoes, unpeeled

3 ounces green beans (about 10)

Boston or leaf lettuce

½ cup canned white albacore tuna packed in water, drained

½ tomato, cut into 4 wedges

1 hard-cooked egg, halved lengthwise

2 whole black olives

Chopped parsley

Vinaigrette Dressing (see recipe)

Boil potatoes for 15 to 20 minutes or until tender. Drain; cut in half. Blanch beans in boiling water for 2 minutes, until bright green and crisp-tender. Drain.

Line a salad plate with lettuce; place tuna in center of the plate. Arrange tomato wedges on one side, then egg and olives. Place warm potatoes on tuna; top with warm green beans. Sprinkle with parsley. Serve with dressing on the side.

VINAIGRETTE DRESSING

Yield: about ½ cup

1 small clove garlic, crushed

½ teaspoon kosher salt

1 teaspoon Dijon mustard

1½ tablespoons lemon juice

2 teaspoons red wine vinegar

¼ teaspoon ground black pepper

⅓ cup olive oil

Combine garlic and salt in a small bowl; mash together with the back of a spoon until the mixture forms a paste. Stir in mustard, lemon juice, vinegar and pepper. Drizzle in oil, whisking constantly until well blended.

SALAD PER SERVING
calories 385 • fat 9.5g • % calories from fat 22 • saturated fat 2.5g • cholesterol 254mg • protein 36g • carbohydrate 39g • sugar 3.5g • fiber 5.5g • sodium 534mg • calcium 92mg • potassium 692mg

DRESSING PER TABLESPOON
calories 83 • fat 9g • % calories from fat 98 • saturated fat 1g • cholesterol 0 • protein 0 • carbohydrate 0.5g • sugar 0 • fiber 0 • sodium 128mg • calcium 1mg • potassium 6mg

SALMON FRITTERS WITH LEMON-CAPER SAUCE

Yield: 2 servings

2 boneless, skinless salmon fillets (1 pound total)

Kosher salt

Freshly ground black pepper

1/2 cup mayonnaise

1 egg white

2 tablespoons minced green bell pepper

2 tablespoons minced red bell pepper

2 green onions, minced

2 tablespoons minced fresh parsley

2 tablespoons minced fresh basil

1 tablespoon lemon juice

1 dash Tabasco sauce

1/4 teaspoon ground red (cayenne) pepper

1/4 teaspoon curry powder

1/2 teaspoon minced fresh dill

1/2 cup fine dried bread crumbs

1 tablespoon coarse-grain mustard

1/4 cup roasted corn relish (see note)

Olive oil

1 shallot, minced

1/2 cup white wine

2 tablespoons lemon juice

2 tablespoons capers

1/4 cup (1/2 stick) unsalted butter, cut into 4 pieces

Prepare a medium-hot fire in the grill. Season fillets with salt and pepper to taste. Grill until almost cooked through. Let cool.

In a large mixing bowl, fold together mayonnaise, egg white, bell peppers, green onions, parsley, basil, lemon juice, Tabasco, cayenne, curry powder, dill, bread crumbs, mustard and corn relish. Gently break up salmon fillets into mixture. Fold to combine. Cover; refrigerate at least 2 hours.

Form mixture into 10 large balls. Heat a small amount of olive oil in a skillet over medium-high heat. Place about 5 salmon balls in the skillet. Flatten slightly. Cook until lightly browned, about 3 minutes per side. Repeat with remaining salmon balls. Set fritters aside.

To make the sauce, immediately add a little oil and minced shallots to the skillet. Quickly sauté shallots, then add wine. Bring to a boil; cook until liquid is reduced by about two-thirds. Add lemon juice, capers and pepper to taste. Remove from heat; slowly whisk in butter, 1 tablespoon at a time. Season to taste with salt. Serve sauce over fritters.

Note: To prepare the relish, stir together 1 1/2 cups roasted fresh corn kernels or thawed frozen corn plus 1 teaspoon liquid smoke; 2 tablespoons chopped roasted red bell pepper; 2 chopped green onions; 2 tablespoons chopped red onion; 1 tablespoon chopped basil; 1 small serrano chile, chopped; 1 tablespoon lime juice; 1/2 cup olive oil; 2 teaspoons balsamic vinegar; 1/2 teaspoon granulated garlic; 1 tablespoon granulated sugar; and salt to taste. Let sit for 2 hours or refrigerate overnight. Yield: About 2 cups.

SALMON FRITTERS PER SERVING
calories 1,171 • fat 89g • % calories from fat 68 • saturated fat 24g • cholesterol 186mg • protein 54g • carbohydrate 35g • sugar 5g • fiber 4g • sodium 1,087mg • calcium 196mg • potassium 1,194mg

ROASTED CORN RELISH PER 1/2-CUP SERVIING
calories 336 • fat 28.5g • % calories from fat 76 • saturated fat 4g • cholesterol 0 • protein 2g • carbohydrate 18g • sugar 5g • fiber 2g • sodium 4mg • calcium 12mg • potassium 186mg

GRILLED MAHI-MAHI WITH LEMON AND BASIL AIOLI

Yield: 8 servings

1 tablespoon lemon juice

2 teaspoons diced shallot

1 teaspoon chopped garlic

1 teaspoon Dijon mustard

1 egg (see note)

2 tablespoons chopped basil leaves

²/₃ cup olive oil, plus more for fish

Salt

Ground pepper

Honey, optional

8 (6- to 8-ounce) mahi-mahi fillets

To make the aioli, combine lemon juice, shallot, garlic, mustard and egg in a blender; process until well mixed. Add basil; blend for a few seconds to chop well. With blender running on low, add ²/₃ cup olive oil in a slow stream. Add salt and pepper to taste. If aioli is too acidic, blend in honey to taste. Set aside.

Prepare a hot fire in the grill. Rinse fish; pat dry. Rub fish with olive oil; season to taste with salt and pepper. Grill 4 minutes on each side. (Total cooking time should be about 10 minutes per inch of thickness.)

Serve fish with a dollop of aioli on top.

Note: If uncooked eggs are a health concern, use eggs pasteurized in the shell, sold under the Davidson's brand. Another option is to add the lemon juice, mustard and minced basil to 1 cup commercial mayonnaise, then add honey to taste.

ER SERVING

lories 319 • fat 20.5g • % calories from fat 58 • saturated fat 3g • cholesterol 154mg • protein 32.5g • carbohydrate 1g • sugar 0 • fiber 0 • sodium 175mg • calcium 31mg • potassium 725mg   95

PARMESAN-CRUSTED SOLE

Yield: 2 servings

FOR FISH:

1 cup all-purpose flour

1 egg

1/2 cup milk

1 cup fine dry bread crumbs

1 cup freshly grated Parmesan cheese

1 teaspoon granulated garlic or garlic powder

1 pinch salt

1 teaspoon ground pepper

1 tablespoon chopped fresh parsley

2 (6-ounce) sole fillets

1/4 cup vegetable oil

FOR SAUCE:

1 cup white wine

1 shallot, chopped

Juice of 1/2 lemon

1/4 cup (1/2 stick) cold unsalted butter, cut into small pieces

1 tablespoon capers

Salt

Ground pepper

Lemon slices, for garnish

To prepare fish: Place flour in a shallow dish; whisk egg into milk in a second dish. In a third dish, stir together bread crumbs, cheese, garlic, salt, pepper and parsley.

Coat fillets with flour, dip in egg wash, then coat with crumb mixture. Heat oil in a large skillet over moderate heat. Sauté fillets until golden, about 3 minutes a side. Drain on paper towels. Set aside; keep warm.

Meanwhile, prepare sauce: In a small saucepan, combine wine, shallot and lemon juice over high heat; bring to a boil and cook until reduced to about 1/4 cup. Remove from heat; whisk in butter, capers and salt and pepper to taste.

Place fillets on serving plates; top with sauce. Garnish with lemon slices.

PER SERVING

calories 1,129 • fat 49g • % calories from fat 39 • saturated fat 25g • cholesterol 288mg • protein 68g • carbohydrate 98g • sugar 8g • fiber 4g • sodium 1,625mg • calcium 823mg • potassium 1,090mg   97

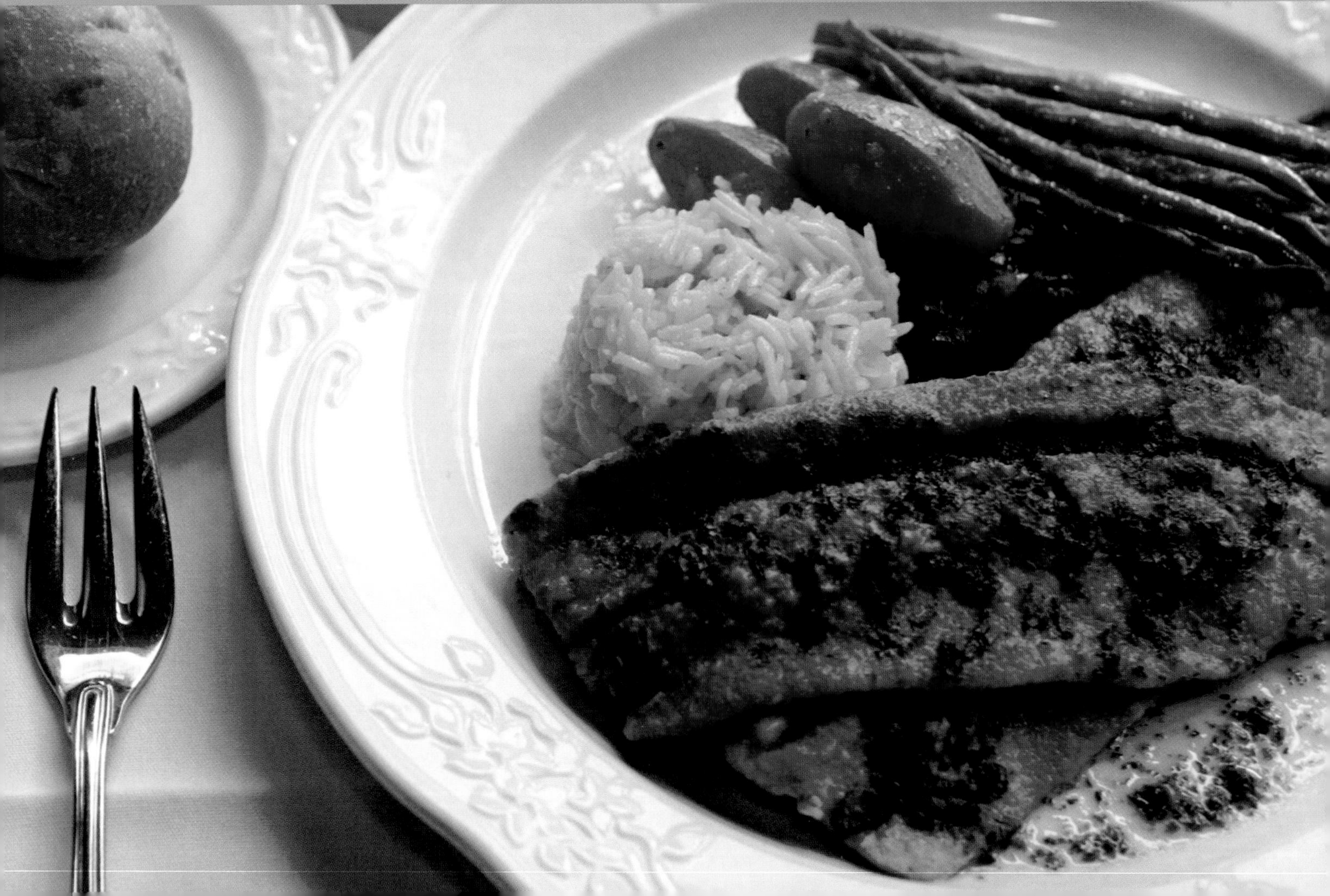

TROUT MEUNIÈRE

Yield: 4 servings

4 whole trout (about 12 ounces each) or 4 trout fillets (7 to 8 ounces each)

Kosher salt

¼ cup all-purpose flour

¼ cup clarified butter (see note) or 2 tablespoons olive oil plus 2 tablespoons butter

2 tablespoons fresh lemon juice

¼ cup (½ stick) butter

2 tablespoons chopped fresh parsley, tarragon, cilantro or chervil

Lemon wedges, for garnish

If using whole trout, remove heads; clean fish and pat dry. Carefully remove fins; fillet the fish, leaving skin intact. Remove the row of small pin bones from fillets with tweezers or a sharp knife.

Lightly salt flesh side of fillets; dip both sides in flour and shake off any excess.

Heat a sauté pan on high; when hot, add clarified butter and reduce heat to medium-high. Immediately add trout, flesh side down, and cook about 4 minutes, until lightly browned. Turn fish over and turn off heat; the hot pan will finish cooking the thin fillets. After another 4 minutes, transfer fish to a serving platter; set aside and keep warm.

Pour off any liquid from the pan; add lemon juice and ¼ cup butter. Place the pan over medium heat until butter becomes frothy; add the herb of your choice. Pour over fish, garnish with lemon and serve immediately.

Variations: For Trout Grenbloise, add about 2 teaspoons drained capers with the chopped herbs. For Trout Amandine, add 3 to 4 tablespoons sliced almonds to the frothy butter.

Note: To clarify butter, melt stick of butter, let cool, then chill. Lift off the solids and discard the white liquid. Melt the solidified butterfat again for easy measuring.

PER SERVING

Calories 528 • fat 37g • % calories from fat 63 • saturated fat 14g • cholesterol 162mg • protein 42g • carbohydrate 7g • sugar 0.5g • fiber 0.5g • sodium 342mg • calcium 95mg • potassium 750mg

SHELLFISH SAUSAGE

Yield: 16 (3-inch) sausages (about 2 pounds)

½ **pound fresh (preservative-free) scallops**

¾ **pound shrimp (preferably rock or bay), peeled and deveined**

¼ **pound lump blue crabmeat**

4 slices smoked bacon, coarsely chopped

3 egg whites

¾ **cup (1½ sticks) unsalted butter, softened**

1 cup chopped leeks (white part only)

2 tablespoons slivered basil

½ **red bell pepper, roasted**

2¼ teaspoons ground coriander

1 tablespoon minced garlic

1½ teaspoons grated orange zest (colored portion of peel)

Kosher salt

Freshly ground black pepper

1 (4-foot-length) pork casing (see note)

6 cups chicken broth or shellfish stock

Combine seafood, bacon, egg whites, butter, leeks, basil, bell pepper, coriander, garlic and orange zest; run through a sausage grinder or pulse in food processor until combined. Place in a large, chilled bowl; mix in salt and pepper to taste. Sauté about 1 tablespoon of the mixture and taste; adjust seasoning.

Run through sausage grinder again with casing attached, or pipe into casing with a pastry bag. Twist and tie sausage at 3-inch intervals; chill.

Bring stock to a simmer; poke sausage several times with small paring knife, and poach in stock for 10 minutes. Remove to a large bowl nestled in a larger bowl filled with ice water; let cool completely. (Extra sausage may be frozen.)

Serving suggestion: Make a vinaigrette with rice wine vinegar and olive oil, adding minced ginger, minced garlic and soy sauce or tamari for flavor. Toss together a salad of frisée, baby spinach, toasted pistachios, shaved fennel and orange sections. Sauté sausages in a small amount of olive oil just to warm, about 2 minutes. Arrange 1 or 2 sausages on each salad; drizzle with the vinaigrette.

Note: Pork casings are sold at many meat markets.

PER SAUSAGE
calories 254 • fat 11g • % calories from fat 39 • saturated fat 6g • cholesterol 109mg • protein 31.5g • carbohydrate 5g • sugar 0.5g • fiber 0.5g • sodium 417mg • calcium 63mg

CRAWFISH CAKES WITH CAJUN AIOLI

Yield: 4 servings

FOR AIOLI:

¾ cup mayonnaise

⅓ cup Thousand Island dressing

¼ cup finely chopped parsley

2 teaspoons Cajun seasoning

1 tablespoon fresh lemon juice

1½ teaspoons fresh lime juice

FOR CRAWFISH CAKES:

1 pound frozen crawfish meat

3 eggs, divided

¼ cup diced yellow bell pepper

¼ cup diced red bell pepper

½ cup finely diced Spanish onion

¼ cup plus 1 cup all-purpose flour, divided

5 tablespoons Italian-seasoned dry bread crumbs

2 tablespoons Cajun seasoning

2 tablespoons Dijon mustard

2 tablespoons finely chopped fresh cilantro

1 cup olive oil

To prepare aioli: Whisk together mayonnaise, Thousand Island dressing, parsley, Cajun seasoning, lemon juice and lime juice. Cover and refrigerate until needed.

To prepare crawfish cakes: Thaw crawfish. Strain liquid from meat; set liquid aside in a medium bowl. Squeeze as much additional liquid from the crawfish meat as possible; add to the bowl. (You will need 2 tablespoons liquid.)

Beat 1 egg in a large bowl. Add crawfish meat, bell peppers, onion, ¼ cup flour, bread crumbs, Cajun seasoning, mustard and cilantro; mix gently but thoroughly. Form into 8 cakes, each about 1 inch thick and 2 to 3 inches in diameter.

Divide the remaining 1 cup flour between 2 shallow bowls. Whisk together the remaining 2 eggs and the 2 tablespoons liquid from the crawfish in a third bowl. Coat both sides of each cake in flour, then in egg wash, then in flour from the second bowl.

Heat oil in a medium frying pan over medium-high heat. Add cakes to pan, working in batches if necessary; cook until golden brown on both sides, about 2 minutes per side.

Drizzle aioli over the crawfish cakes and serve.

Note: If you prefer, you can eliminate the three-step breading process and deep-frying. Simply dust the cakes with flour, place them on a cooling rack and refrigerate for 30 minutes to 1 hour. To cook the cakes, pan-fry in about ¼ to ½ cup olive oil over medium-high heat.

PER SERVING
calories 860 • fat 64g • % calories from fat 67 • saturated fat 9.5g • cholesterol 310mg • protein 28g • carbohydrate 43g • sugar 5g • fiber 2g • sodium 1,954mg • calcium 87mg • potassium 533mg

SAUTÉED SCALLOPS WITH CHARDONNAY SAUCE

Yield: 6 servings

¼ cup (½ stick) butter

1 large shallot, diced

1 pound mushrooms, sliced

1 cup Chardonnay or other
   dry white wine

3 cups heavy cream

Salt

Freshly ground white pepper

Sprigs of dill or rosemary

1 (14-ounce) can artichoke
   hearts, drained, optional

1½ pounds large sea
   scallops

All-purpose flour

Vegetable oil

Melt butter in a large skillet over medium heat. Add shallot and mushrooms; sauté just until shallot is soft and mushrooms are tender. Add wine; simmer until liquid is reduced by half. Add cream; simmer until mixture thickens, about 8 minutes. (Sauce should lightly coat the back of a spoon.)

Season to taste with salt and white pepper. Add several sprigs of herbs and artichokes. Taste sauce and adjust seasoning; set aside and keep warm.

Dust scallops with flour; shake off excess. Lightly coat a large skillet with oil and place over medium-high heat. When oil is hot, add scallops in batches. Cook until lightly browned on both sides, wiping pan clean and adding oil after each batch.

To serve, ladle sauce onto warmed dinner plates. Arrange scallops on sauce; garnish with additional herb sprigs.

PER SERVING
calories 674 • fat 57g • % calories from fat 76 • saturated fat 33g • cholesterol 221mg • protein 25g • carbohydrate 12g • sugar 3.5g • fiber 1.5g • sodium 231mg • calcium 111mg • potassium 765mg

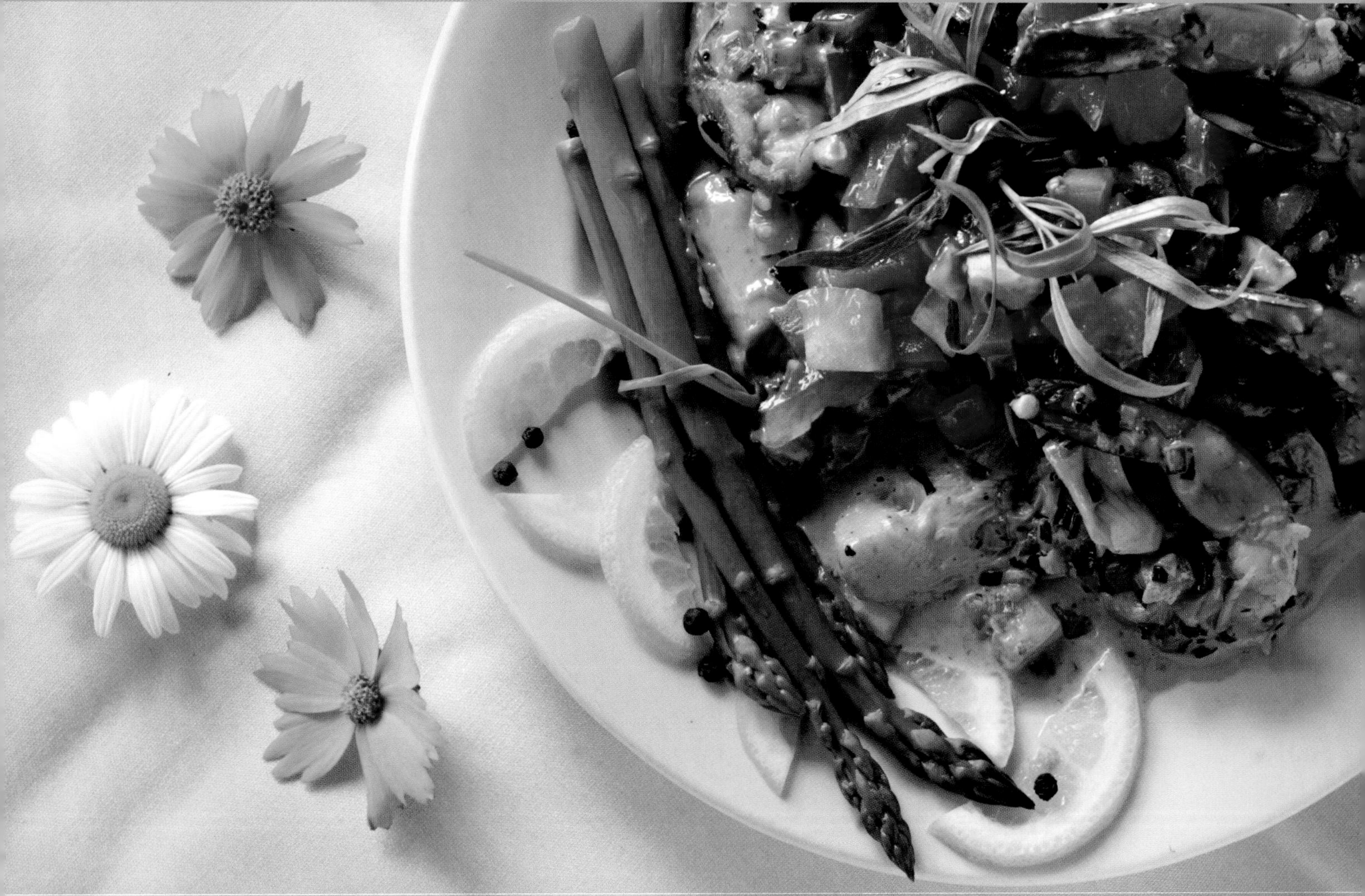

SHRIMP SARA

Yield: 1 serving

FOR BASIL BUTTER (SEE NOTE):

2 ounces fresh basil

1 cup (2 sticks) butter, softened

FOR SHRIMP:

6 tablespoons chopped green onion (about 3 onions)

½ teaspoon minced fresh garlic or to taste

¾ cup sliced fresh mushrooms

6 to 8 large (16 to 20 count) shrimp, peeled and deveined

⅛ teaspoon dried tarragon

Salt

Coarsely ground pepper

2 tablespoons warm brandy

¼ cup sweet white Port (such as Gallo's Fairbanks)

4 to 6 tablespoons heavy cream

3 tablespoons seeded, diced tomato

2 canned artichoke hearts, drained and quartered

To prepare butter: Pick basil leaves from stems; process leaves briefly in food processor. Add softened butter; blend well. Set aside.

To prepare shrimp: In a medium skillet, sauté green onion, garlic and mushrooms in 2 tablespoons basil butter until vegetables are tender. Add shrimp; season with tarragon and salt and pepper to taste. Cook over medium heat, turning shrimp frequently, until three-fourths done, about 3 minutes. Add brandy, then carefully touch a lighted match to the brandy. Shake the pan until the flame dies. Add Port; simmer 2 or 3 minutes or until liquid has reduced by half, removing shrimp when done and setting them aside.

Add cream to pan; cook to reduce sauce to a smooth, creamy texture, 2 to 3 minutes. Pour any liquid off tomatoes. Add tomatoes, artichoke hearts and shrimp to the skillet; cook just until warmed through. Serve immediately.

Note: Basil butter keeps for two weeks in the refrigerator or several months in the freezer. You will need 2 tablespoons for this recipe. Use the rest instead of plain butter in soups, in pasta or with vegetables.

Tester's note: This dish goes well with a side of small pasta, such as orzo or anellini; the sauce turns the pasta into a gourmet treat.

PER SERVING

calories 461 • fat 33.5g • % calories from fat 65 • saturated fat 20g • cholesterol 194mg • protein 16.5g • carbohydrate 17g • sugar 8g • fiber 3g • sodium 292mg • calcium 118mg • potassium 592mg

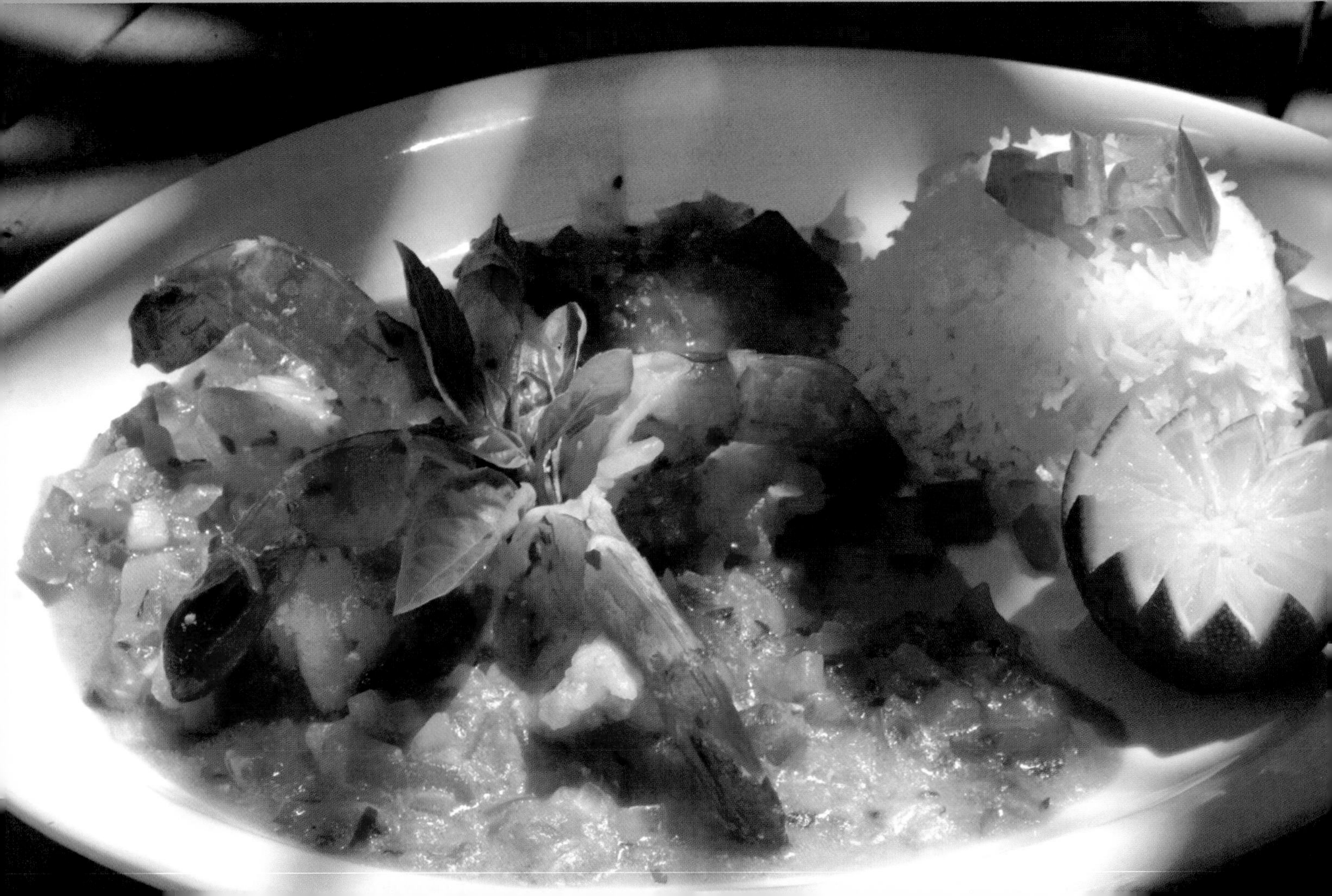

BOBO DE CAMARAO YEMANJA

Yield: 4 servings (about 1⅓ cups each)

½ pound yuca, peeled and coarsely chopped (see note)

Salt

1½ cups diced sweet onion

2½ tablespoons olive oil

1 tablespoon tomato paste

2 medium tomatoes, diced

1½ pounds medium shrimp, peeled and deveined

½ bunch cilantro, chopped (about 1 cup)

½ teaspoon minced fresh hot pepper of your choice

1 cup canned coconut milk (not sweetened)

¼ cup fish stock (see note)

Ground white pepper

Cooked rice

Place yuca in a saucepan; cover with cold water. Add ½ teaspoon salt. Bring to a boil, then cook until tender, about 12 minutes. Drain, mash and set aside.

In a large skillet, sauté onion in olive oil until translucent. Add tomato paste and fresh tomatoes; cook over medium heat 5 minutes. Add shrimp, cilantro and hot pepper; stir in coconut milk, mashed yuca and fish stock. Cook until reduced to a thick, creamy consistency, about 7 minutes; add salt and white pepper to taste. Serve with rice.

Note: Yuca (also called yucca, cassava or manioc root) is sold at Latin American markets. Instead of fish stock, you can use bottled clam juice or "seafood base" (concentrated bouillon available in specialty stores) dissolved in water according to package directions.

PER SERVING
alories 466 • fat 24g • % calories from fat 46 • saturated fat 12.5g • cholesterol 259mg • protein 37.5g • carbohydrate 25g • sugar 5g • fiber 3g • sodium 417mg • calcium 125mg • potassium 811mg

GRINDERS

Yield: 4 servings

FOR GRINDER SAUCE:

11 tablespoons butter, divided

3 tablespoons all-purpose flour

1 cup water

¼ cup hot-pepper sauce (the restaurant uses Frank's Cayenne Pepper Sauce)

1½ teaspoons chicken base (concentrated broth sold near canned soups)

½ teaspoon Cajun seasoning

FOR SANDWICHES:

4 (8-inch) pieces French bread

2 pounds raw oysters, shucked, or about 24 ounces small cooked shrimp, or about 24 ounces diced cooked chicken

To prepare sauce: First, make a roux. Melt 3 tablespoons butter. Stir in flour until well-mixed. Set aside.

In a medium saucepan, mix together water, pepper sauce, chicken base and Cajun seasoning; bring to a boil. Whisk in roux and cook until thickened. (Mixture will be quite thick). Remove from heat; stir in remaining 8 tablespoons butter.

To prepare sandwiches: Using a long, serrated knife, slice bread in half lengthwise. Hollow out bread, leaving a 1-inch border.

In a skillet, combine about ⅓ cup sauce and oysters; cook over medium heat just until plumped, 2 to 3 minutes depending on size. (If using cooked shrimp or chicken, stir into ⅓ cup sauce and cook just until heated through.) Spoon filling and remaining sauce into hollowed-out bread; serve immediately.

PER SERVING

calories 637 • fat 39g • % calories from fat 55 • saturated fat 22g • cholesterol 207mg • protein 23g • carbohydrate 47g • sugar 1g • fiber 2g • sodium 1,674mg • calcium 169mg

111

NORTON'S CAFE 808 Geyer Avenue • St. Louis • 314-436-0828 • www.nortonscafe.com

JAMBALAYA

Yield: 15 cups

1 medium onion, chopped

2 green bell peppers, chopped

3 ribs celery, chopped

⅓ cup plus 2 tablespoons granulated sugar

4 ounces Norton's Cajun seasoning
(about 1 cup; see tester's note)

2 cups (4 sticks) margarine

1 pound raw chicken, cut into bite-size pieces
(about 2 cups)

3 cups hot water

3 cups tomato sauce or canned diced tomatoes

10 ounces andouille sausage, cut into bite-size
pieces (2 cups)

10 ounces ham, cut into bite-size pieces
(2 cups)

1½ tablespoons beef base (sold near the
bouillon and broths in many supermarkets)

2½ cups uncooked white rice

In a large pot, combine onion, bell peppers, celery, sugar, seasoning and margarine. Cook over low heat until margarine is melted.

Add chicken; cook for about 3 minutes. Add hot water, tomato sauce, sausage, ham, beef base and rice. Stir well, cover with a tight-fitting lid and simmer for about 30 minutes or until rice is cooked, stirring 4 or 5 times to prevent sticking. Add water near the end of cooking if extra liquid is needed.

Tester's note: You can purchase Norton's Cajun seasoning at the restaurant. We substituted 1 tablespoon of Paul Prudhomme's Magic Seasoning Blend for Vegetables. Despite the difference in the amounts, the substitution worked well.

PER (1½-CUP) SERVING
alories 755 • fat 49g • % calories from fat 58 • saturated fat 624g • cholesterol 54mg • protein 24g • carbohydrate 55g • sugar 14g • fiber 2.5g • sodium 3,621mg • calcium 55mg • potassium 624mg   113

STEAK SALAD

Yield: 4 servings

FOR STEAK:

1 tablespoon olive oil

1 tablespoon minced celery

1 tablespoon minced carrot

1 tablespoon minced shallots

1 cup white wine

1 bay leaf

1 tablespoon honey

1 tablespoon Worcestershire sauce

1 tablespoon light soy sauce

1 tablespoon Dijon mustard

1 tablespoon balsamic vinegar

Zest (grated portion of peel) and juice of 1 lemon

1 tablespoon mixed chopped herbs (parsley, thyme and rosemary)

1¼ pounds beef tenderloin, cut into ½-inch cubes

FOR SALAD:

8 ounces mixed baby greens

8 ounces sliced mushrooms

8 thin slices red onion, separated into rings

Balsamic vinaigrette (see recipe)

8 ounces crumbled blue cheese

To prepare steak: First, make the marinade. Heat olive oil in medium skillet over medium-high heat. Add celery, carrot and shallots; sauté for 2 to 4 minutes or until vegetables soften. Pour in wine; add bay leaf. Let mixture simmer until reduced by half.

Add honey, Worcestershire sauce, light soy sauce, mustard, vinegar, lemon zest, lemon juice and chopped herbs. Whisk together until blended. Let cool. Prepare a fire in the grill or preheat the broiler.

Thread beef pieces onto metal skewers. Dip meat into marinade for a few seconds. Grill or broil until done to taste.

To prepare salad: Divide greens among four dinner plates. Top greens with mushrooms and onion.

Remove meat from skewers and arrange on salads. Drizzle balsamic vinaigrette over all. Top with crumbled blue cheese. Serve immediately.

BALSAMIC VINAIGRETTE

Yield: About 1 cup

¾ cup olive oil

¼ cup balsamic vinegar

1 tablespoon Dijon mustard

Whisk olive oil, vinegar and mustard together until well-blended.

PER SERVING (without dressing)
calories 561 • fat 36g • % calories from fat 58 • saturated fat 18g • cholesterol 138mg • protein 43g • carbohydrate 14.5g • sugar 7g • fiber 3g • sodium 981mg • calcium 369mg • potassium 974mg

DRESSING PER TABLESPOON
calories 98 • fat 10.5g • % calories from fat 96 • saturated fat 1.5g • cholesterol 0 • protein 0 • carbohydrate 1g • sugar 1g • fiber 0 • sodium 13mg • calcium 1mg • potassium 4mg

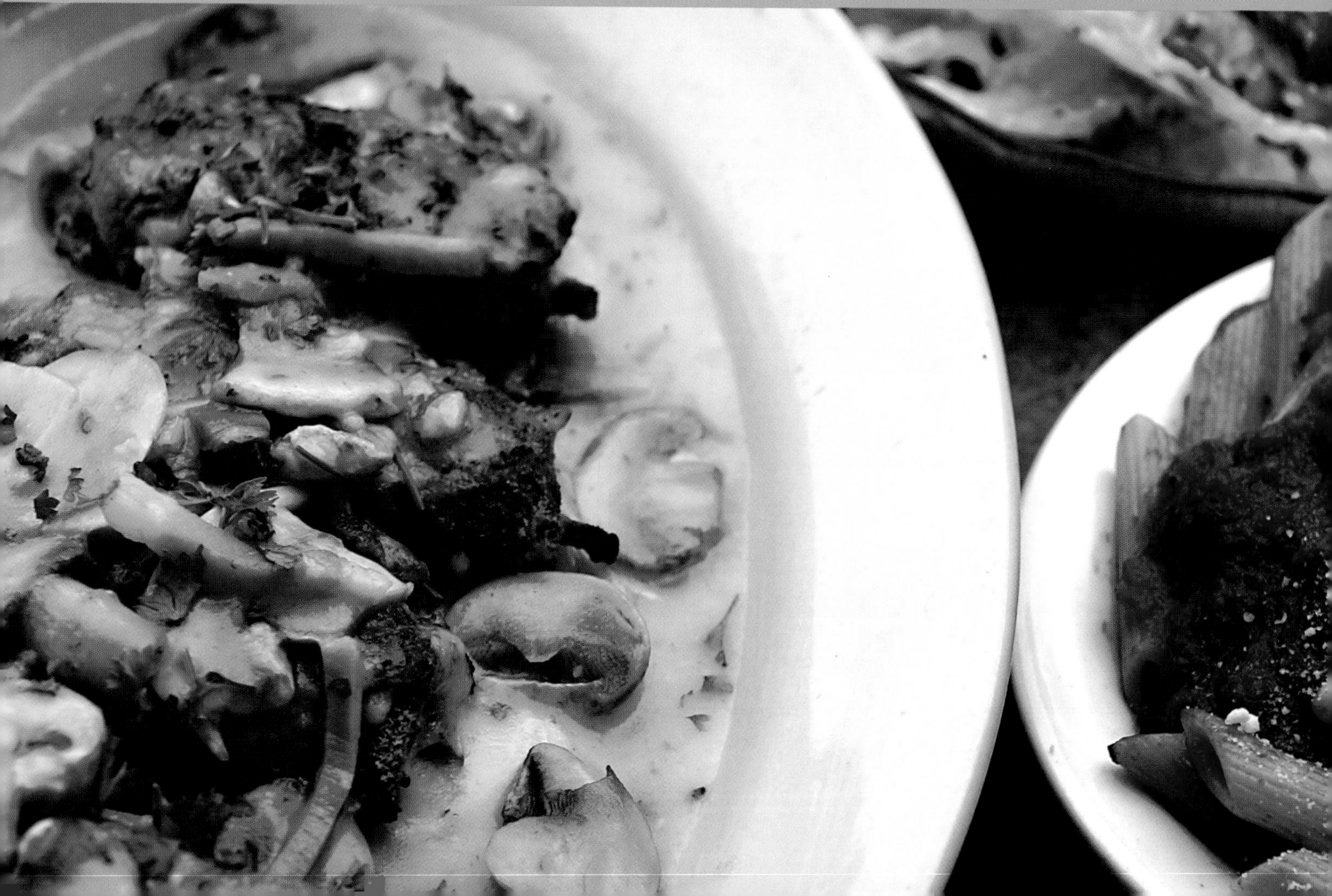

TENDERLOIN SPIEDINI

Yield: 1 serving

FOR SAUCE:

1 tablespoon butter

1 tablespoon all-purpose flour

1/2 cup chicken stock

2 tablespoons dry white wine

1 tablespoon lemon juice

1/2 cup sliced mushrooms

FOR SPIEDINI:

4 (1 1/2- to 2-ounce) pieces beef tenderloin

Olive oil, for brushing

1/4 cup Italian-seasoned dry bread crumbs, divided

2 (1/4-inch-thick) slices prosciutto, chopped; divided

1/3 cup shredded mozzarella or provolone cheese

Chopped fresh parsley, for garnish

To prepare sauce: Melt butter; stir in flour until well-blended, making a roux.

In a skillet, blend stock, wine and lemon juice. Place over medium heat. Whisk in roux. Cook, whisking constantly, until thickened. Add mushrooms; cook about 3 minutes, stirring frequently. Keep warm.

To prepare spiedini: Preheat grill or broiler to high heat.

Gently flatten each piece of tenderloin to about 1/8 inch thick (about 4 inches square). Brush one side of each piece of tenderloin with oil; sprinkle lightly with bread crumbs. Set aside about 1 tablespoon prosciutto; distribute remaining prosciutto over beef. Divide cheese evenly over prosciutto. Roll up each beef slice tightly; secure with a skewer. Brush rolls with olive oil, and sprinkle lightly with bread crumbs.

Grill to desired doneness or broil about 4 inches from heat for 5 to 6 minutes, turning every 2 minutes. Arrange on a serving plate; top with sauce. Garnish with parsley and reserved prosciutto.

PER SERVING
calories 832 • fat 40g • % calories from fat 43 • saturated fat 18g • cholesterol 196mg • protein 60g • carbohydrate 58g • sugar 6g • fiber 2g • sodium 1,969mg • calcium 392mg • potassium 721mg

ZANTI'S TRATTORIA Former owner Roberto Zanti owns Roberto's Trattoria, 145 Concord Plaza in south St. Louis County.

FILET ZANTI

Yield: 1 serving

FOR STEAK:

Salt

Ground black pepper

1 (8-ounce) filet mignon

1 tablespoon olive oil or truffle oil

About ½ cup dried bread crumbs

1 tablespoon butter

1 slice mozzarella cheese

FOR SAUCE:

½ cup sliced fresh mushrooms

3 tablespoons butter, divided

2 tablespoons white wine

6 tablespoons beef stock

Juice from ½ lemon

1 to 2 tablespoons all-purpose flour

To prepare steak: Prepare a hot fire in the grill. Salt and pepper filet to taste. Drizzle with oil. Roll in bread crumbs. Place pat of butter atop filet; place meat on grill. Grill to desired doneness. Just before removing from grill, melt mozzarella cheese on top.

To prepare sauce: Sauté mushrooms in 1 tablespoon butter for about 1 minute. Add wine, beef stock and lemon juice. Bring to a boil.

Roll remaining 2 tablespoons butter in flour to coat thoroughly. Add to sauce; cook for a few more minutes, until thickened.

Place filet on plate. Pour sauce over meat. Serve immediately.

PER SERVING
calories 1,346 • fat 97g • % calories from fat 65 • saturated fat 46g • cholesterol 288mg • protein 62g • carbohydrate 51g • sugar 5.5g • fiber 3g • sodium 818mg • calcium 361mg • potassium 1,003mg

HAWTHORNE INN 123 Front Street • Labadie, Mo. • 636-451-0004 • and • 3 Prairie Dell Plaza • Union, Mo. • 636-583-6677

MUSHROOM CHEESE STEAK

Yield: 4 servings

1 teaspoon dried thyme or to taste

1 teaspoon garlic powder or to taste

1 teaspoon salt or to taste

2 teaspoons ground black pepper or to taste, divided

4 (12-ounce) strip steaks

2 cups beef broth

2 teaspoons minced shallots

2 cups sliced mushrooms

2 tablespoons margarine

2 tablespoons all-purpose flour

8 slices provolone cheese

Preheat the broiler or grill. Mix thyme, garlic powder, salt and 1 teaspoon pepper; season steaks on both sides. Broil or grill steaks to desired doneness.

While steaks are cooking, place a large skillet over high heat; add beef broth and remaining 1 teaspoon pepper. Bring to a boil. Add shallots and mushrooms; reduce heat slightly and cook until mushrooms are tender, about 6 minutes.

In a small pan, melt margarine. Stir in flour until blended to make a roux; stir roux into broth mixture. (If sauce is too thick, add water to desired consistency.)

When steaks are done, place 2 slices cheese on top of each; arrange on serving plates. Top with hot sauce.

PER SERVING
calories 757 · fat 40.5g · % calories from fat 48 · saturated fat 18g · cholesterol 186mg · protein 91g · carbohydrate 7g · sugar 1g · fiber 1g · sodium 1,696mg · calcium 505mg · potassium 1,180mg

LOW-COUNTRY MEAT PIES

Yield: 6 servings

¾ **pound ground beef**

¼ **pound pork sausage links, casings removed**

2 **tablespoons chopped garlic**

½ **cup chopped yellow onion**

1 **teaspoon salt**

1 **teaspoon ground black pepper**

1 **teaspoon dried basil**

1 **tablespoon Worcestershire sauce**

1 **teaspoon celery salt**

1 **teaspoon ground dried thyme**

1 **teaspoon rosemary leaves**

3 **sheets puff pastry, thawed (see note)**

Vegetable oil, for deep-frying

Ranch dressing, for serving (see note)

In a medium skillet, combine beef, sausage, garlic, onion, salt, pepper, basil, Worcestershire, celery salt, thyme and rosemary. Sauté until browned, about 7 minutes, breaking up the meat as it cooks so that no large pieces remain. Drain; discard fat. Let meat mixture cool.

Cut each sheet of puff pastry into four 5-inch squares; cover and refrigerate until ready to use.

Spoon about ¼ cup meat mixture into the center of each pastry square. Fold pastry over the meat to form a triangle; press edges together tightly with the tines of a fork.

Bring oil to 350 degrees in a deep-fryer or Dutch oven. Cook one or two pastries at a time, holding them down with slotted spoons to keep the pastry immersed in oil. Deep-fry about 4 minutes or until golden brown. Drain for a moment on paper towels. Serve hot with ranch dressing.

Notes: A 17.3-ounce box of frozen puff pastry contains 2 sheets. You will need 1½ boxes for this recipe. Store the remaining pastry in a sealable plastic bag in the freezer.

Tin Can Tavern serves these with its Smoked Tomato Bacon Ranch Dressing; home cooks can use a favorite prepared ranch dressing.

PER SERVING

calories 796 • fat 52g • % calories from fat 59 • saturated fat 9g • cholesterol 35mg • protein 22g • carbohydrate 60g • sugar 2g • fiber 2.5g • sodium 1,048mg • calcium 37mg • potassium 168mg

LoRusso's

VEAL SALTIMBOCCA

Yield: 4 servings

4 (4- to 5-ounce) veal cutlets

3 tablespoons all-purpose flour

Salt

Freshly ground black pepper

6 tablespoons (3/4 stick) cold butter, divided

2 to 4 tablespoons extra-virgin olive oil

4 thin slices Volpi prosciutto

4 thin slices fontina cheese

6 ounces mushrooms, thickly sliced

6 fresh sage leaves, divided

1/2 cup dry white wine

1/2 cup chicken stock

Place each cutlet between 2 sheets of plastic wrap; pound very thin. Season flour to taste with salt and pepper. Dredge (lightly coat) cutlets in seasoned flour.

Melt 4 tablespoons butter in a heavy skillet over high heat; add 2 tablespoons oil. Sauté veal, 1 to 2 minutes on each side, until just brown. (Cook in batches if necessary to prevent crowding in the pan, adding the remaining 2 tablespoons oil as needed.) Remove veal to a warm platter. Top veal with prosciutto, then cheese; set aside and keep warm.

Reduce heat to medium. Add mushrooms and 2 sage leaves to the skillet; sauté about 3 minutes. Stir in wine, scraping the pan to loosen any caramelized pieces. Add chicken stock and stir well; simmer until reduced by half, about 4 minutes. Add salt and pepper to taste. Add remaining 2 tablespoons cold butter; swirl pan to melt butter and thicken sauce slightly. Pour hot sauce over veal; place one whole sage leaf on each serving. Serve immediately.

PER SERVING

Calories 597 • fat 46g • % calories from fat 69 • saturated fat 21g • cholesterol 180mg • protein 36g • carbohydrate 7.5g • sugar 1g • fiber 1.5g • sodium 541mg • calcium 135mg • potassium 439mg

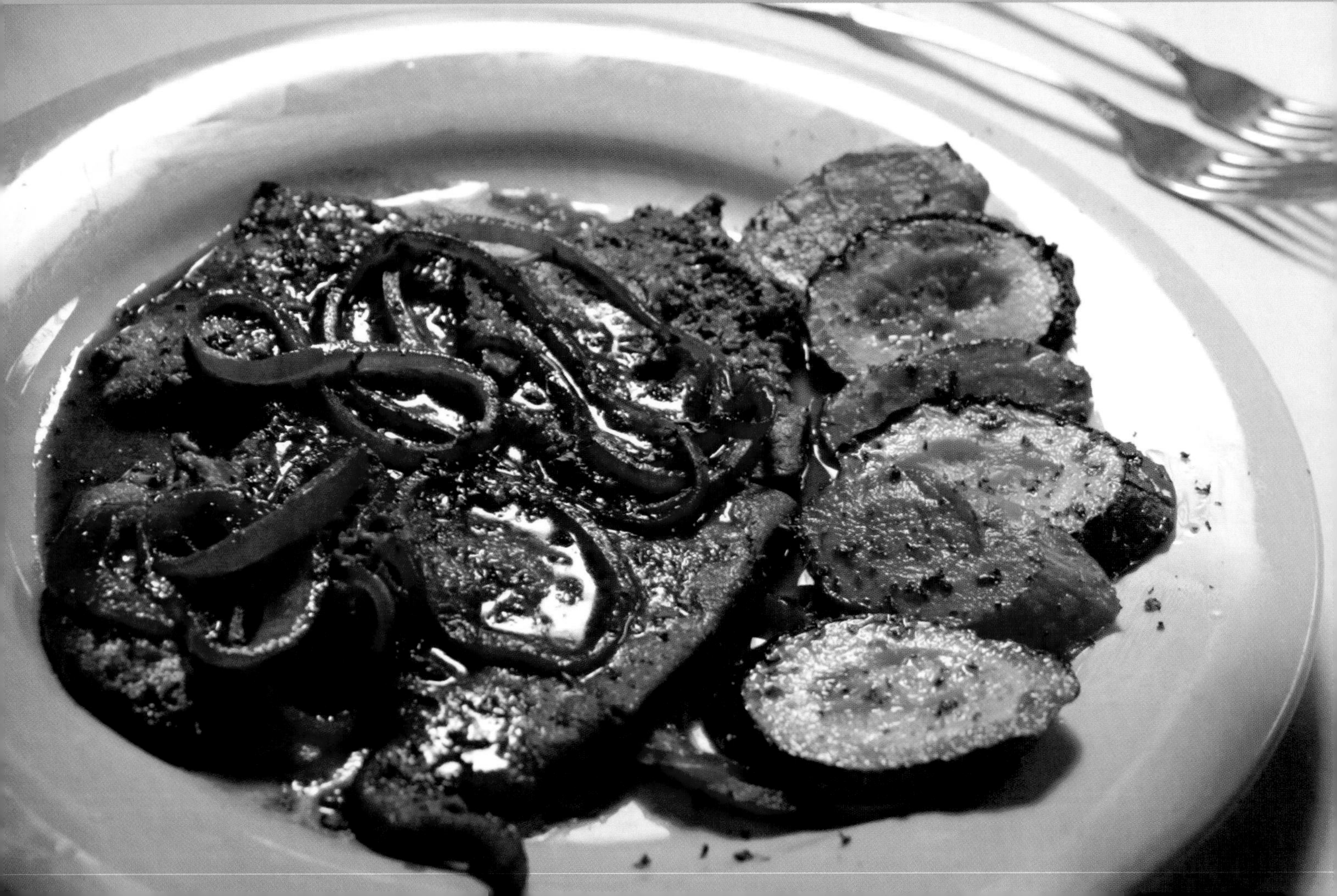

LIVER SWEET AND SOUR

Yield: 2 servings

3 tablespoons extra-virgin olive oil

1 medium red onion, thinly sliced (about 1½ cups)

2 to 3 sprigs parsley, finely chopped, divided

8 ounces calf's liver (4 pieces, each about ⅓ inch thick)

All-purpose flour

Salt

Freshly ground pepper

2 tablespoons red-wine vinegar

1 tablespoon balsamic vinegar

¼ cup Port

2 to 4 tablespoons beef broth, optional

2 teaspoons unsalted butter

Heat oil in a large skillet over medium heat. As soon as the oil starts to bubble, add onion and half of the parsley. Cover, reduce heat to low and cook until onion is soft and lightly browned, about 7 minutes. Push onion to the side of the pan; increase heat slightly.

Lightly coat liver with flour. Add liver to skillet; cook about 3 minutes on each side, just to brown. Add salt and pepper to taste, then vinegars and Port; simmer for 2 minutes. Sauce should be thin; if too thick, add beef broth. Add butter, stirring until melted. Sprinkle with remaining parsley and serve hot.

MAIN DISHES

PER SERVING

calories 478 • fat 30g • % calories from fat 56 • saturated fat 7g • cholesterol 361mg • protein 22g • carbohydrate 22g • sugar 8g • fiber 1g • sodium 79mg • calcium 31mg • potassium 478mg

127

GRILLED PRAIRIE GRASS FARMS LAMB CHOPS IN ASIAN APRICOT GLAZE

Yield: 8 servings

1 tablespoon grapeseed oil

1 shallot, minced

1 cup diced fresh apricots or apricot preserves

½ cup white wine

¾ cup teriyaki sauce

Grated zest (colored portion of peel) and juice of 3 large lemons (about 6 tablespoons of juice)

1 pinch ground red (cayenne) pepper

Salt

Ground black pepper

8 (13- to 16-ounce) racks of lamb (see note)

Vegetable oil, for grill

In a 2-quart saucepan, heat grapeseed oil over medium heat; add shallot and cook until translucent. Add apricots or preserves. Pour in the wine, stirring with a wooden spoon to loosen any browned bits from the saucepan. Add teriyaki, lemon zest and juice. Bring to a simmer; cook 20 minutes. Season with cayenne and salt and pepper to taste. Let cool.

Remove fat cap (thick fat layer on back of bones) and silver skin from lamb; cut each rack into two-chop portions. Marinate in the apricot glaze for 1 hour at room temperature. Heat grill (see tester's note). Brush hot grill with vegetable oil. Remove lamb from marinade; season to taste with salt and pepper. Sear for about 1 minute on each side, then grill to desired doneness, 8 to 10 minutes for medium-rare.

Note: Grass-fed lamb raised near New Florence, Mo., can be purchased by calling Prairie Grass Farms at 573-835-2272.

Tester's note: Lamb may be seared on each side in a sauté pan on top of the stove, then roasted on an oiled rack in a preheated 425-degree oven.

PER SERVING
calories 460 • fat 26g • % calories from fat 51 • saturated fat 11g • cholesterol 178mg • protein 55g • carbohydrate 1.5g • sugar 1g • fiber 0 • sodium 389mg • calcium 37mg • potassium 700mg

129

SUNSET 44 BISTRO 118 West Adams Avenue • Kirkwood, Mo. • 314-965-6644 • www.sunset44.com

PORK TENDERLOIN WITH CRANBERRY GINGER CHUTNEY

Yield: 6 servings pork; 5 cups chutney

FOR CHUTNEY:

2 (12-ounce) bags fresh cranberries

1 pound (3 cups lightly packed) brown sugar

1½ cups currants

1 cup dried apricots, quartered

1 teaspoon ground cinnamon

⅛ teaspoon ground red (cayenne) pepper

1 cup cranberry juice

1 tablespoon plus 1 teaspoon minced fresh ginger

FOR PORK:

Nonstick cooking spray

¼ cup soy sauce

¾ cup Burgundy wine

1 tablespoon dried oregano, crushed

1 teaspoon garlic powder plus more to taste

¼ cup corn oil

2 pounds pork tenderloin, excess fat and silver skin removed

Salt

Ground black pepper

To prepare chutney: Combine cranberries, sugar, currants, apricots, cinnamon, cayenne, cranberry juice and ginger in a heavy saucepan. Cook over medium heat, stirring until sugar is dissolved. Increase heat to high; boil 10 minutes. Pour into a bowl. (Refrigerate leftovers in an airtight container.)

To prepare pork: Preheat oven to 350 degrees; place a cake rack over a shallow baking pan (such as a jellyroll pan), and coat the rack with cooking spray.

Combine soy sauce, wine, oregano and 1 teaspoon garlic powder in a bowl; slowly whisk in oil to emulsify. Add pork; marinate 10 minutes at room temperature (or refrigerate overnight). Drain pork, discarding marinade. Season pork with salt, pepper and garlic powder to taste. Arrange pork on prepared rack; roast to an internal temperature of 165 degrees, about 35 minutes.

Let pork stand about 5 minutes, then slice ½ inch thick. Spoon some warm chutney onto each serving plate; arrange pork slices on top.

PER SERVING (with ¼ cup chutney)
calories 363 • fat 9.5g • % calories from fat 24 • saturated fat 3g • cholesterol 100mg • protein 33g • carbohydrate 34.5g • sugar 30g • fiber 2g • sodium 334mg • calcium 40.5mg • potassium 685mg

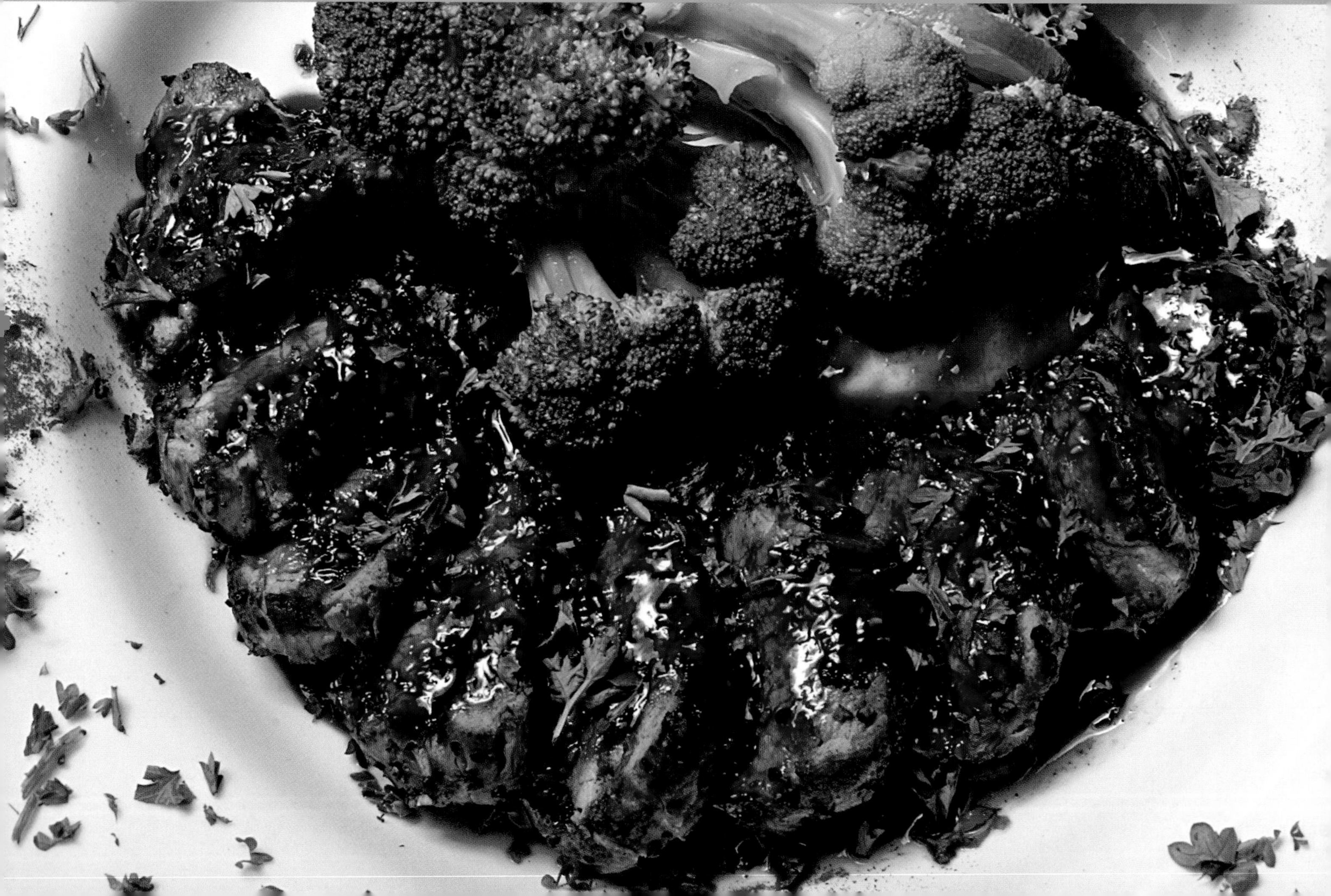

PORK TENDERLOIN WITH RASPBERRY SAUCE

Yield: 4 servings

2 cups vegetable oil

3 tablespoons honey

2 tablespoons soy sauce

2 tablespoons onion powder

4 (8-ounce) pieces pork tenderloin, silver skin removed

2 tablespoons Lawry's seasoned salt

¼ cup cracked black pepper

Raspberry sauce (see recipe)

To make a marinade, whisk together oil, honey, soy sauce and onion powder. Place tenderloin in a resealable plastic bag; add marinade, seal and refrigerate overnight.

The next day, discard marinade. Sprinkle tenderloin with seasoned salt and pepper. Preheat grill. Warm the raspberry sauce.

Cook tenderloin 2 minutes on each side. Slice each tenderloin into 6 medallions, then grill medallions for another 30 seconds on each side. (Pork is safely cooked when internal temperature reaches 160 degrees. Medallions may still be slightly pink inside.) Serve sauce over medallions.

RASPBERRY SAUCE

Yield: 2 cups

18 ounces raspberry preserves (about 1½ cups)

¼ cup red wine vinegar

2 tablespoons soy sauce

1½ teaspoons prepared horseradish

1½ teaspoons ketchup

1 tablespoon garlic powder

Combine ingredients; whisk to combine.

PER SERVING (without sauce)
alories 326 • fat 11.5g • % calories from fat 32 • saturated fat 3g • cholesterol 147mg • protein 48.5g • carbohydrate 5g • sugar 0.5g • fiber 1.5g • sodium 2,414mg • calcium 36mg

AUCE PER TABLESPOON
alories 40 • fat 0 • saturated fat 0 • cholesterol 0 • protein 0 • carbohydrate 10.5g • sugar 5g • fiber 0 • sodium 93mg • calcium 1mg

CHIMICHANGA MEXICAN RESTAURANT 5425 South Grand Boulevard • St. Louis • 314-352-0202

CHILE VERDE

Yield: 6 servings

FOR PORK CARNITAS:

1 (4- to 5-pound) pork shoulder (butt)

2 cups water

3 tablespoons vegetable oil

1/4 cup chopped garlic

1 tablespoon salt

3 or 4 basil leaves, chopped

Juice of 3 lemons

3/4 cup regular cola (not diet)

3/4 cup orange juice

3/4 cup dark Mexican beer

3/4 cup milk

FOR GREEN SALSA (CHILE VERDE):

1 or 2 fresh jalapeños

1 or 2 dried red chiles

1 (15-ounce) can tomatillos (available at ethnic markets)

1 medium yellow onion, cut into 1/2-inch pieces

3 tablespoons chopped garlic

1 tablespoon salt

1 bunch cilantro, stems trimmed and discarded

To prepare pork carnitas: Preheat oven to 475 degrees. Grease a roasting pan; line with parchment paper. Place a roasting rack in the pan. Place pork, fat side up, on the roasting rack. Pour 2 cups water into the pan. Roast for 45 minutes, then reduce heat to 325 degrees and roast for 5 hours or until you can easily pull the meat just above the rack off the roast with a fork.

Let cool for 30 minutes. Pull off strips of pork; chop the strips into 1- to 2-inch chunks. (You will need 2 pounds of cooked pork for this recipe; refrigerate or freeze any remainder for another use.)

Heat oil over medium-high heat in a large skillet or pot that you can cover with a lid. Add 2 pounds chopped pork; sauté for 5 minutes. Add garlic, salt, basil and lemon juice; simmer for 5 to 10 minutes.

Add cola, orange juice and beer; cover and simmer until tender, about 1½ hours, adding milk during the final 10 minutes.

To prepare green salsa (chile verde): Place jalapeños and red chiles in a small saucepan; cover with water, bring to a boil and simmer until soft, about 20 to 25 minutes. Drain. Stem jalapeños and red chiles; chop red chiles into ½-inch pieces.

Drain tomatillos, reserving the liquid. Transfer tomatillos to a food processor or blender; add softened chiles, onion, garlic, salt and cilantro. Process until finely chopped, adding reserved tomatillo liquid as needed or desired.

To serve: Divide pork mixture among serving plates; spoon salsa over pork. Serve with soft corn or flour tortillas.

PER SERVING
calories 512 • fat 27.5g • % calories from fat 48 • saturated fat 8g • cholesterol 147mg • protein 43g • carbohydrate 20.5g • sugar 9g • fiber 2g • sodium 2,501mg • calcium 83mg • potassium 943mg

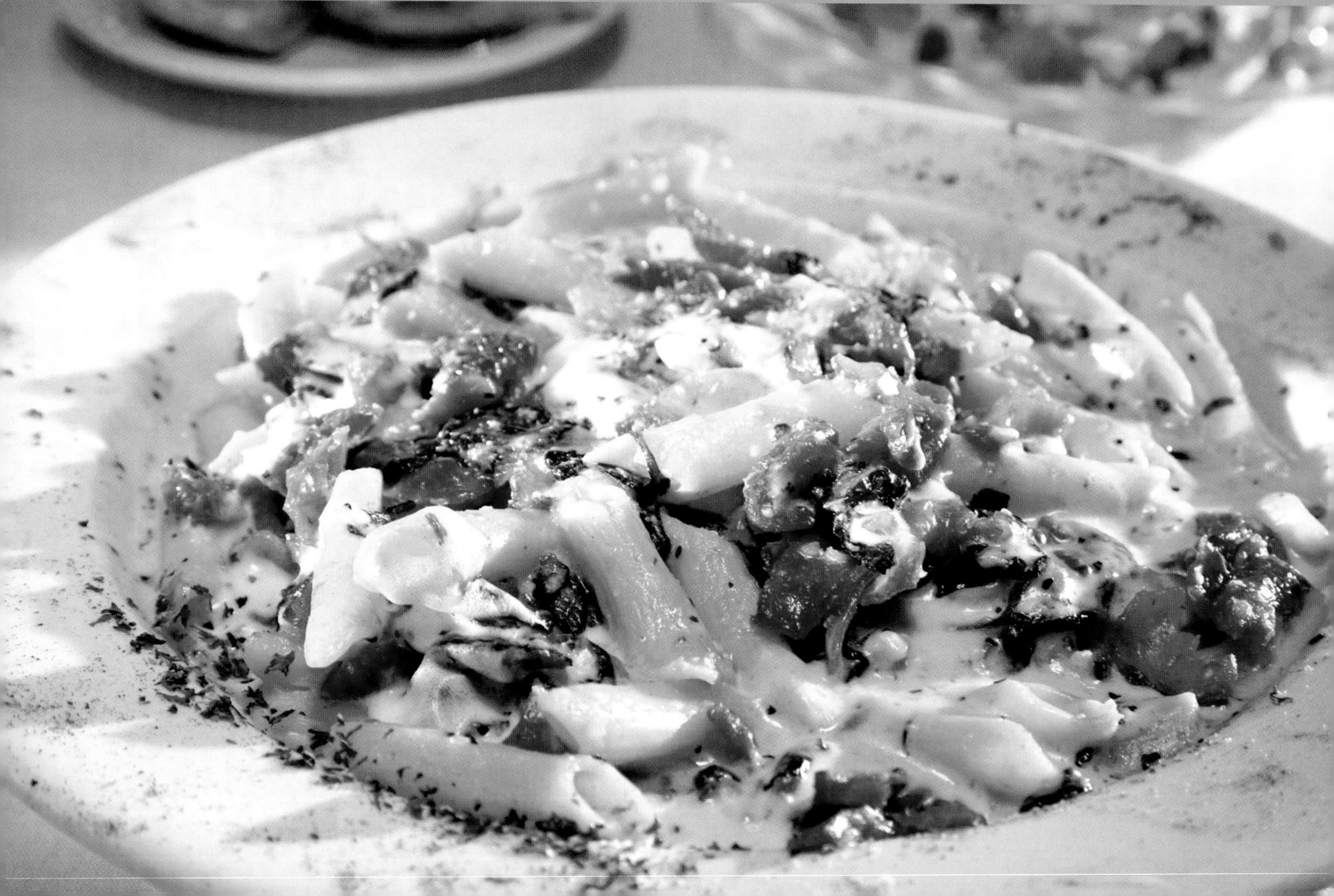

BLT PASTA

Yield: 4 servings

½ pound bacon

Cracked black pepper

3 cups half-and-half

2 tablespoons butter

1 pinch red pepper flakes

3 to 4 cups baby spinach

¾ cup chopped sun-dried tomatoes

2 tablespoons chopped garlic

About ¾ cup grated Parmesan cheese

Salt

Ground black pepper

1 pound fettuccine, cooked and drained

Preheat oven to 350 degrees. Arrange slices of bacon on a parchment-lined baking sheet. Sprinkle with cracked pepper to taste; bake until crisp, 15 to 20 minutes. Drain on paper towels and let cool. Chop bacon.

To make a sauce, combine half-and-half, butter and red pepper flakes in a large pot; cook over medium heat, stirring often, until butter melts.

In a large skillet, combine spinach, chopped bacon, tomatoes and garlic; cook over medium-high heat, tossing, until spinach begins to wilt. Add spinach mixture to sauce; bring to a boil. Gradually stir in Parmesan; cook until sauce thickens. Add salt and ground pepper to taste. Add cooked pasta; toss well.

PER SERVING
calories 933 • fat 43g • % calories from fat 41 • saturated fat 22.5g • cholesterol 117mg • protein 38.5g • carbohydrate 98g • sugar 8g • fiber 6g • sodium 1,114mg • calcium 552mg • potassium 918mg

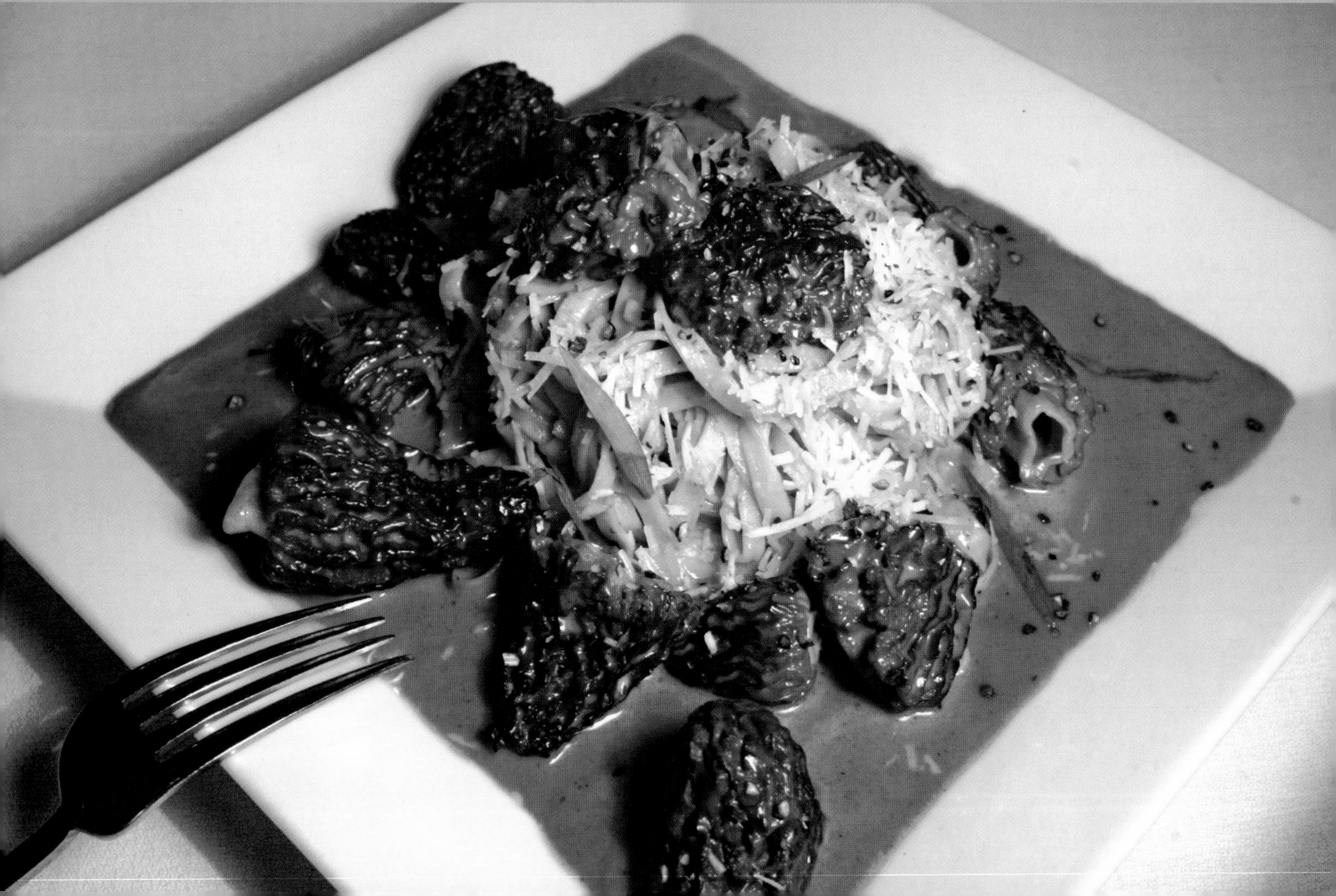

MOREL MUSHROOM PASTA

Yield: 2 servings

FOR SAUCE:

2 cups heavy cream

1/4 cup plus 2 tablespoons ruby Port

1 1/2 teaspoons red wine vinegar

Salt

Freshly ground pepper

FOR PASTA:

7 ounces egg linguine (see note)

5 ounces fresh morel mushrooms (see note)

2 tablespoons butter

1/2 teaspoon salt or to taste

1/4 teaspoon freshly ground pepper or to taste

Fresh tarragon, for garnish

Pecorino Romano cheese, for garnish

Cracked black pepper, for garnish

To prepare sauce: In a medium saucepan, combine cream and Port; simmer over medium heat until reduced by half, about 15 minutes. Transfer to a blender; add vinegar and salt and pepper to taste. Process for 10 seconds. Set aside and keep warm. (Yield: About 1 1/4 cups sauce.)

To prepare pasta: Cook linguine according to package directions.

Meanwhile, place mushrooms in a bowl; working quickly, cover with water, swish to remove soil and drain well. If water is very dirty, repeat and drain well. Wrap mushrooms in a dry towel; shake vigorously to remove as much moisture as possible.

In a large skillet, sauté mushrooms in butter; season with salt and pepper. Add 1/2 cup warm sauce to pan. (Reserve remaining sauce for another use.) Add linguine; toss to combine.

Place pasta on serving plates; garnish with tarragon, cheese and pepper.

Notes: Many forms of egg pasta are available in markets and specialty stores. Those most like the pasta used in this recipe are the home-style egg noodles, narrow-cut and relatively thick (similar in size to standard linguine, but not as long).

Fresh morels are in season for a short time each spring. They are sometimes available at specialty stores and farmers markets.

PER SERVING
calories 625 • fat 33.5g • % calories from fat 48 • saturated fat 19.5g • cholesterol 179mg • protein 15g • carbohydrate 66g • sugar 3g • fiber 3g • sodium 631mg • calcium 70mg • potassium 380mg

RIGATONI WITH EGGPLANT

Yield: 6 servings

1 pound rigatoni

⅓ cup olive oil

1 small eggplant (about 1 pound), peeled and diced

4 cloves garlic, minced

¼ cup large capers

⅓ cup sliced pitted kalamata olives

1 cup white wine

2 cups tomato sauce

Leaves from 3 sprigs basil, slivered

½ teaspoon salt or to taste

¼ teaspoon ground black pepper or to taste

8 ounces fresh mozzarella, cut in half-dollar-size slices

Cook rigatoni according to package directions; drain, set aside and keep warm.

Heat oil in a large skillet. Add eggplant; sauté until golden brown. Add garlic, capers and olives; sauté 30 seconds. Add wine; cook until reduced by half, about 1 minute. Stir in tomato sauce and basil. Season to taste with salt and pepper. Add mozzarella and rigatoni to eggplant mixture, toss and serve.

PER SERVING
calories 595 • fat 24g • % calories from fat 36 • saturated fat 8g • cholesterol 30mg • protein 19g • carbohydrate 69.5g • sugar 9g • fiber 0 • sodium 1,000mg • calcium 260mg • potassium 597mg

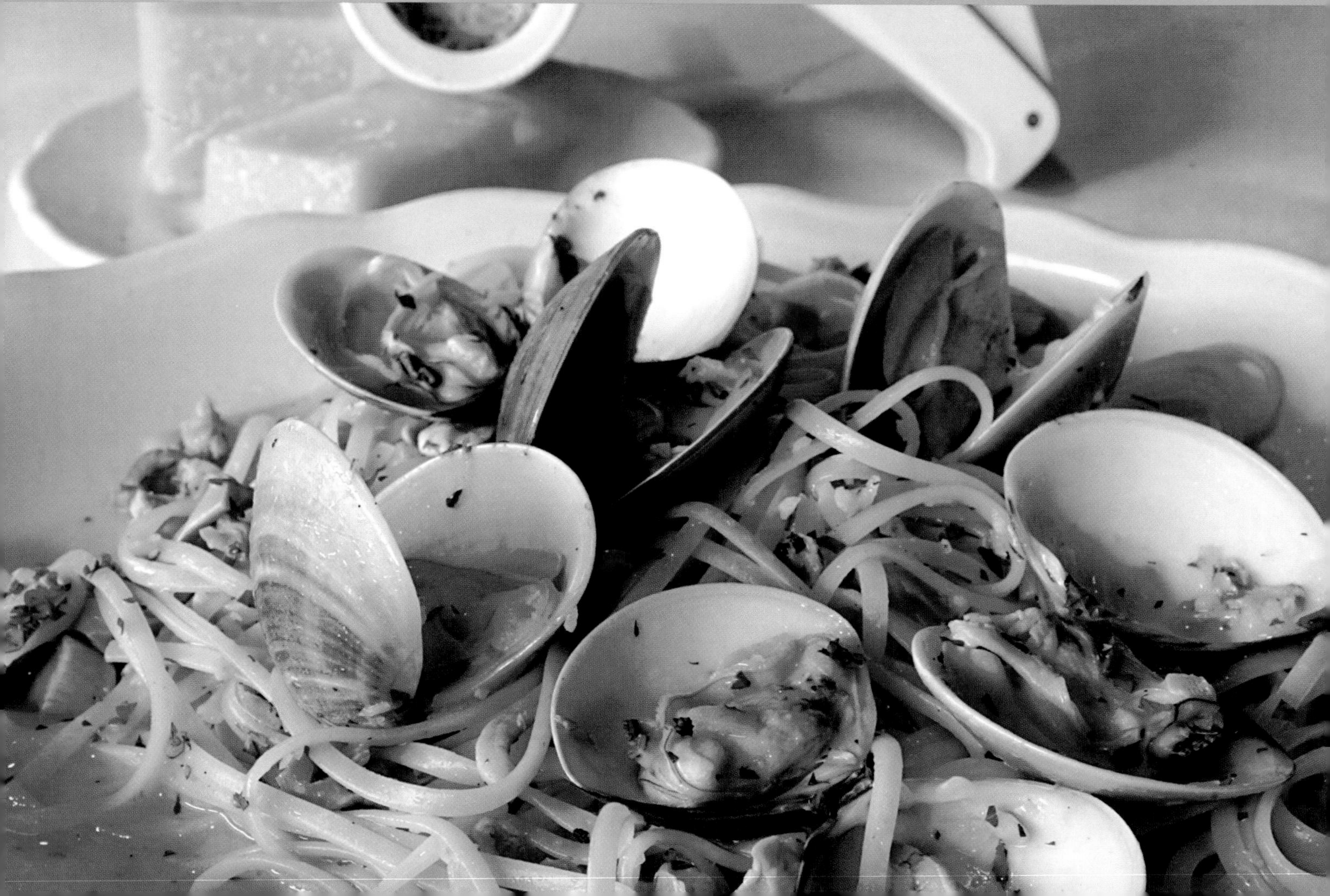

LINGUINE WITH CLAMS

Yield: 4 servings

1 pound linguine

¼ cup olive oil

24 small cherrystone or littleneck clams, scrubbed clean

6 cloves garlic, chopped

1 (6½-ounce) can chopped clams, undrained

½ cup dry white wine

1 pinch dried red pepper flakes

Ground black pepper

Kosher salt

¼ cup (½ stick) unsalted butter

2 tablespoons chopped Italian parsley

Bring a large pot of water to a boil; cook pasta until al dente. Drain.

As pasta cooks, heat olive oil in a large skillet over medium heat. Add fresh clams; cover and cook 1 to 2 minutes. Stir in garlic; cook, but do not allow garlic to brown. Add chopped clams; cook, uncovered, 1 minute. Add wine, red pepper flakes and pepper and salt to taste.

Add butter; cover pan. Cook until clams have opened (see note). Toss pasta with sauce and parsley. Serve on a large platter, arranging whole clams in their shells around the edge.

Note: When buying fresh clams, check to make sure shells are tightly closed. Fresh clams open as they cook; any clam that does not open during cooking should be discarded.

PER SERVING
calories 724 • fat 29g • % calories from fat 36 • saturated fat 9g • cholesterol 80mg • protein 33g • carbohydrate 81g • sugar 4g • fiber 4g • sodium 293mg • calcium 153mg • potassium 868mg

PENNE BORGHESE

Yield: 4 servings (about 10 cups)

¼ cup extra-virgin olive oil

½ cup finely diced yellow onion

1 cup finely diced prosciutto (about 6 ounces)

½ cup chopped fresh parsley

¼ cup cognac or brandy

1 cup tomato sauce

3 cups heavy cream

¼ teaspoon salt or to taste

⅛ teaspoon ground black pepper or to taste

1 pound penne, cooked according to package directions and drained

½ cup freshly grated Parmigiano cheese, for garnish

Heat oil in a large sauté pan or Dutch oven; add onion, prosciutto and parsley. Cook until onion is translucent, about 2 minutes.

Remove the pan from the heat; add cognac, scraping the bottom of the pan with a wooden spoon to loosen any brown bits. Return the pan to the heat.

Add tomato sauce and cream, stirring until well incorporated; cook to reduce slightly. Add salt and pepper. Add cooked penne; simmer, tossing, until pasta is hot and thoroughly coated. Pour onto a platter and serve immediately, garnished with Parmigiano.

PER SERVING

Calories 1,386 • fat 90.5g • % calories from fat 59 • saturated fat 47g • cholesterol 290mg • protein 35.5g • carbohydrate 104g • sugar 13g • fiber 5.5g • sodium 1,581mg • calcium 287mg • potassium 545mg 145

PASTA CON BROCCOLI

Yield: 2 servings

**4 ounces uncooked pasta
(such as large shells)**

1 cup cream or half-and-half

2 tablespoons butter

½ teaspoon minced garlic

2 tablespoons tomato sauce

½ cup chopped broccoli

Salt

Ground black pepper

⅓ cup sliced mushrooms

**¼ cup grated Parmesan
cheese**

Cook pasta until half done; drain. Return pasta to pot. Add cream, butter, garlic, tomato sauce, broccoli and salt and pepper to taste; bring to a full boil.

When noodles are completely cooked, add mushrooms; stir to combine. Remove from heat; add cheese. Toss and serve.

PER SERVING

Calories 800 • fat 60g • % calories from fat 68 • saturated fat 37g • cholesterol 203mg • protein 17g • carbohydrate 48g • sugar 3g • fiber 3g • sodium 385mg • calcium 303mg • potassium 322mg   147

THAI RED CURRY DRAGONFLY PASTA

Yield: 4 servings

Salt

9 ounces Chinese egg noodles or spaghetti

1 (13-ounce) can unsweetened coconut milk

¼ cup red curry paste (see recipe and note)

½ pound andouille sausage, thinly sliced

2 tablespoons vegetable oil

½ red onion, chopped

2 tablespoons plus 1 teaspoon grated fresh ginger

1 bulb garlic (10 to 12 cloves), chopped

1 carrot, thinly sliced on bias

1 red bell pepper, cut into julienne (matchstick-size) strips

1 yellow or orange bell pepper, cut into julienne strips

1 pound bok choy, chopped

5 ounces blue crabmeat

¼ pound bean sprouts

Bring salted water to a boil; cook noodles until al dente. Set aside.

Bring coconut milk to a boil in a small pot; whisk in curry paste. Remove from heat and set aside.

Heat a wok or deep sauté pan over medium-high heat; sauté sausage until it begins to brown. Add oil, onion, ginger, garlic, carrot, bell peppers and bok choy. Sauté 2 minutes; add crab, bean sprouts and curry mixture, and bring to a boil. Add pasta; simmer 2 minutes, then serve.

Note: Red Moon's chef suggested substituting Mae Ploy brand curry paste if you do not want to make your own.

RED CURRY PASTE

Yield: About 5 tablespoons

4 kaffir lime leaves

12 dried red chiles

5 cloves garlic, peeled and quartered

1 whole shallot (2 pieces), peeled and quartered

1 stalk lemongrass, trimmed and coarsely chopped

Mince lime leaves. Place lime leaves and chiles in a mortar; crush with a pestle until very fine. Transfer mixture to a small food processor; add garlic, shallot and lemongrass. Process until very finely chopped. If mixture does not form a paste, scrape down sides of work bowl and add water, 2 teaspoons at a time, until texture resembles the thickness of tomato paste.

PASTA PER SERVING
alories 719 • fat 39.5g • % calories from fat 49 • saturated fat 22g • cholesterol 48mg • protein 24g • carbohydrate 67g • sugar 5g • fiber 13g • sodium 430mg • calcium 226mg • potassium 896mg
RED CURRY PASTE PER TEASPOON
alories 6 • fat 0 • saturated fat 0 • cholesterol 0 • protein 0 • carbohydrate 1.5g • sugar 0 • fiber 0 • sodium 1mg • calcium 2mg • potassium 13mg

SZECHWAN EGGPLANT

Yield: 2 servings

2 tablespoons granulated sugar

1½ tablespoons Kikkoman soy sauce

2 tablespoons white vinegar

1 tablespoon oyster sauce

1½ tablespoons water

1 teaspoon chopped garlic

½ teaspoon chopped fresh hot chile pepper (such as serrano)

1 (1-pound) eggplant

1 egg

¼ cup plus 1 teaspoon cornstarch, divided

5 cups vegetable oil

1 green onion, chopped

In a large saucepan, whisk together sugar, soy sauce, vinegar, oyster sauce, water, garlic and chile pepper; set aside.

Peel eggplant; cut into 1-by-1-by-2-inch rectangles. Beat egg in a large bowl; add eggplant and toss to coat thoroughly. Sprinkle ¼ cup cornstarch over eggplant; toss to coat eggplant evenly.

In a wok or large skillet, heat oil to medium-high (375 degrees). Add eggplant in a single layer; fry until golden brown on all sides. Remove with a slotted spoon and set aside.

Bring the soy sauce mixture to a boil. In a small dish, mix the remaining 1 teaspoon cornstarch into 1 teaspoon water; stir into the sauce and cook until the mixture thickens, about 1 minute. Add eggplant and green onion; toss to mix well. Serve immediately.

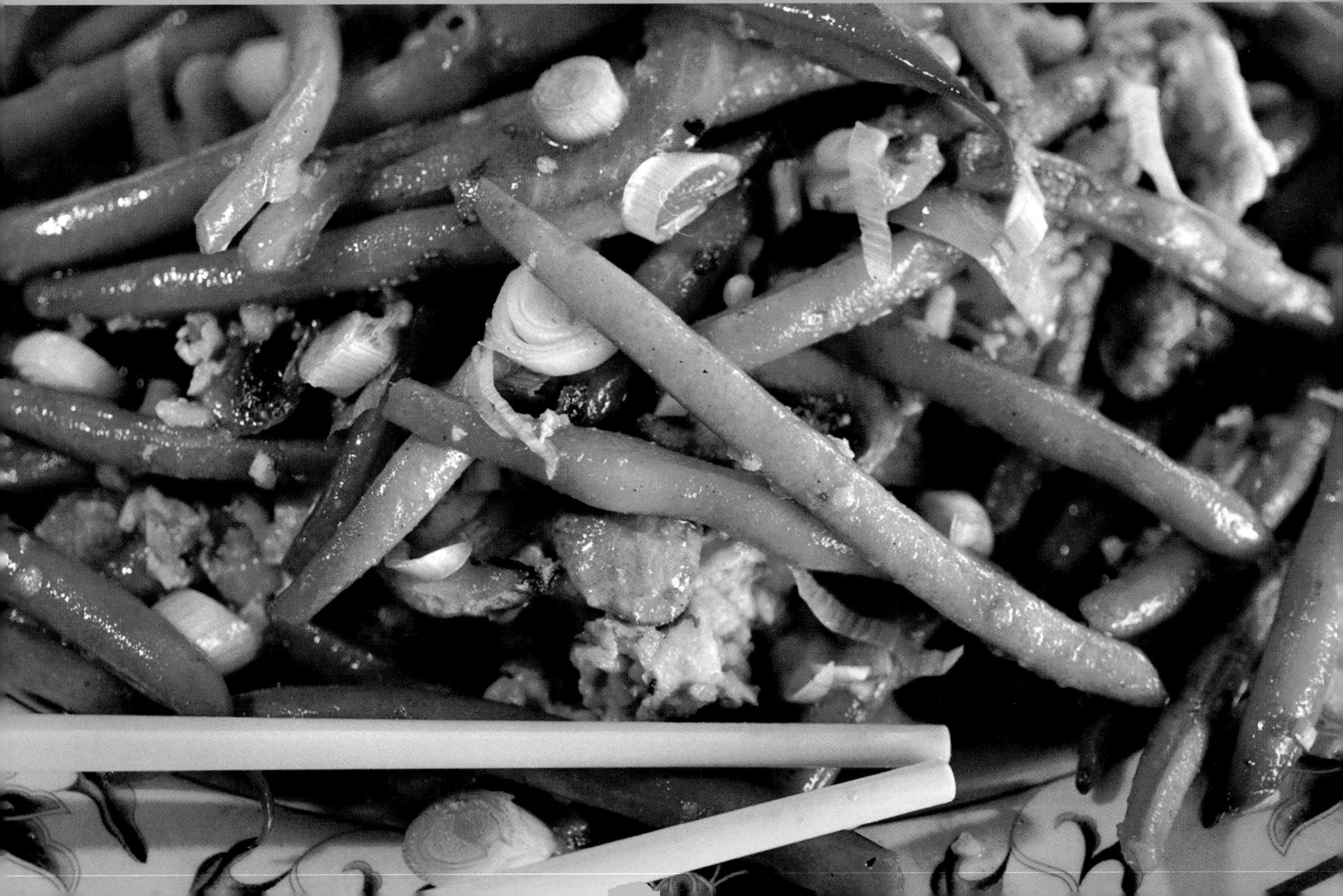

GREEN BEAN AND MUSHROOM STIR-FRY (DAU QUE XAO NAM)

Yield: 4 servings

1 pound green beans, ends removed

¼ pound sliced mushrooms

1 tablespoon vegetable oil

2 cloves garlic, minced

1 cup chicken broth or water

½ cup (1 stick) margarine

1 egg, optional

1½ tablespoons granulated sugar

½ teaspoon salt

½ cup sliced green onion (green and white parts)

Steam green beans over boiling water for 5 to 10 minutes. Add mushrooms; steam 2 to 3 minutes more.

While vegetables are steaming, heat oil in a wok. Add garlic; sauté about 1 minute. Add broth and margarine. Stir until margarine is melted. Crack egg into pan. Stir slowly until egg scrambles.

Stir in sugar and salt. Add green beans, mushrooms and green onion. Cook over medium-high heat until done to taste.

PER SERVING
calories 302 • fat 26g • % calories from fat 77 • saturated fat 4g • cholesterol 1mg • protein 3g • carbohydrate 14g • sugar 7g • fiber 4g • sodium 809mg • calcium 49mg • potassium 317mg

ON THE SIDE

Pear Salad with Cherry Balsamic Vinaigrette • Shrimp and Voodoo Pasta Salad • Cardwell's Grain Salad • Chopped Veggie Salad • Polenta Fries • German Potato Pancakes • Chef Hayden's Carrot Soufflé • Southern Cream Spinach • Farmhouse Bread • Sour Cream Blueberry Bread • Zucchini Bread

PEAR SALAD WITH CHERRY BALSAMIC VINAIGRETTE

Yield: 4 servings

FOR VINAIGRETTE:

3 ounces dried cherries (about ²/₃ cup)

½ cup hot water

2 cloves garlic

¼ cup balsamic vinegar

1 cup extra-virgin olive oil, divided

1 tablespoon Dijon mustard

½ teaspoon salt

½ teaspoon ground white pepper

FOR PEAR SALAD:

6 cups mixed green leaf lettuces

1 cup shredded fontina cheese

2 to 3 green onions (green part only), thinly sliced

½ cup dried cherries

¾ cup Candied Pecans (see recipe)

1 Anjou pear, quartered, cored and sliced

To prepare vinaigrette: Soak cherries in hot water for 15 minutes; pour cherries and liquid into blender container. Add garlic, vinegar and ½ cup olive oil. Process until garlic is finely chopped. Add mustard, salt and pepper, blending after each addition. With blender running, add remaining ½ cup oil in a steady stream. (Makes 2 cups; cover and refrigerate leftovers, and use within a few days.)

To prepare salad: In a bowl, toss lettuce with dressing to taste; divide among 4 serving plates. Sprinkle each salad with cheese, green onions, dried cherries and Candied Pecans, dividing evenly. Arrange pear slices on top of salads.

CANDIED PECANS

Yield: 4 cups

6 cups water

1 pound (4 cups) pecan halves

3 cups vegetable oil, for frying

1 cup powdered sugar, divided

Bring water to a boil in a large pot. Add pecans; boil for 4 to 5 minutes. Pour into a colander and drain thoroughly.

In another deep pot, a wok or an electric deep-fryer, heat oil to 350 degrees.

Scoop about a third of the pecans into a bowl; sprinkle with ⅓ cup powdered sugar, tossing to coat evenly. Scoop sugared pecans into hot oil. Fry until slightly browned, 3 to 4 minutes. Use a slotted spoon to lift nuts from oil onto a baking sheet, arranging nuts in a single layer. (Do not line sheet with paper towels, or pecans will stick.) Repeat with remaining sugar and pecans. Let cool completely.

Note: These pecans will keep for weeks. They make a great addition to many dishes.

PER SERVING (SALAD PLUS ¼ CUP DRESSING)
calories 422 • fat 32g • % calories from fat 68 • saturated fat 7.5g • cholesterol 31mg • protein 10.5g • carbohydrate 23g • sugar 14.5g • fiber 5.5g • sodium 288mg • calcium 221mg • potassium 464mg

PECANS PER ¼-CUP SERVING
calories 247 • fat 21.5g • % calories from fat 78 • saturated fat 2g • cholesterol 0 • protein 2.5g • carbohydrate 11g • sugar 8.5g • fiber 2.5g • sodium 0 • calcium 20mg • potassium 116mg

SHRIMP AND VOODOO PASTA SALAD

Yield: 10 servings

2½ cups uncooked penne pasta

1½ to 2 cups mayonnaise or to taste

1½ teaspoons salt

1½ teaspoons ground black pepper

1½ teaspoons minced garlic

1 tablespoon ground cumin

2½ cups cooked bay shrimp (see note)

3 tablespoons minced jalapeño peppers

¼ cup chopped cilantro

½ cup julienned yellow bell pepper (cut into matchstick-size pieces)

½ cup julienned red bell pepper

1 cup diced tomato

½ cup chopped green onion

1 cup grated Parmesan cheese

Cook pasta according to package directions; drain and let cool.

In a medium bowl, stir together mayonnaise, salt, pepper, garlic and cumin.

In a large bowl, toss together pasta, shrimp, jalapeños, cilantro, bell peppers, tomato and green onion. Add mayonnaise mixture; toss to combine. Chill for 20 minutes. Top with Parmesan; serve.

Note: You can use cooked frozen bay shrimp, which are often called salad shrimp. Thaw according to package directions.

PER SERVING
calories 480 • fat 36.5g • % calories from fat 68 • saturated fat 6g • cholesterol 62mg • protein 11g • carbohydrate 27g • sugar 3g • fiber 3g • sodium 1,029mg • calcium 103mg • potassium 153mg

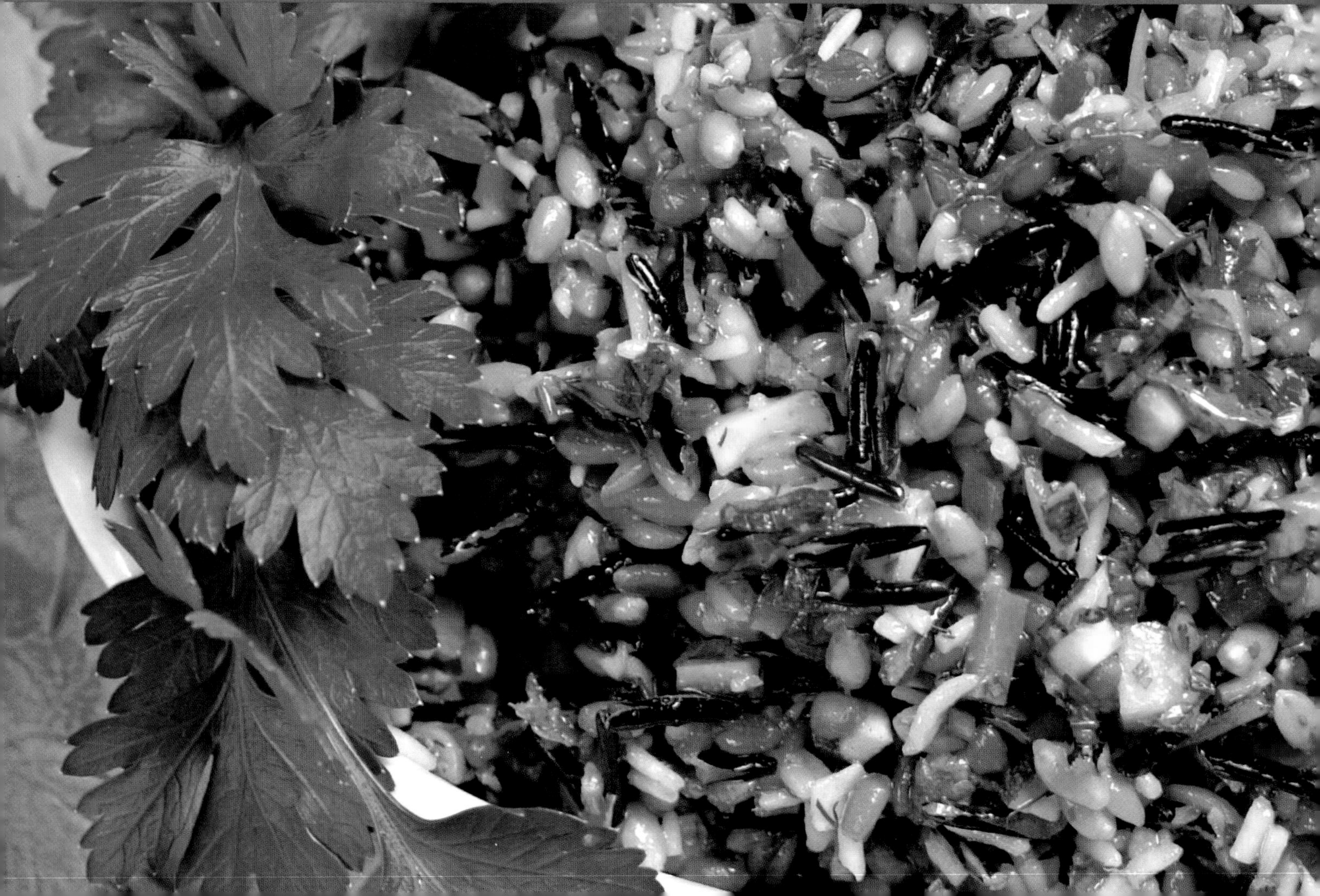

CARDWELL'S GRAIN SALAD

Yield: 8 (1-cup) servings

1 bulb garlic

2/3 cup olive oil, divided

1/4 cup sherry vinegar

3/4 teaspoon sea salt

1/4 teaspoon ground white pepper

1/3 cup finely diced carrots

6 cups cooked grains, drained (see note)

3/4 cup finely diced red bell pepper

3/4 cup finely diced yellow bell pepper

1/3 cup finely diced zucchini

1/3 cup finely diced celery

2 tablespoons minced green onion

2 tablespoons minced parsley

1 tablespoon minced fresh tarragon

1 tablespoon minced fresh dill

Preheat oven to 350 degrees. Separate cloves of garlic from bulb, peel and toss with 1 teaspoon olive oil; place in the center of a piece of aluminum foil. Fold edges together, forming a pouch. Bake 45 to 50 minutes, until garlic is golden brown and very soft. Purée in food processor, or mash with a fork until smooth.

To make the dressing, combine 1½ tablespoons roasted garlic purée with vinegar, salt and pepper. Whisk in remaining olive oil until emulsified.

Cook carrots in boiling water just until crisp-tender; transfer immediately to ice water, then drain well.

Toss together cooked grains, carrots, bell peppers, zucchini, celery, green onion, parsley, tarragon and dill; add dressing to taste. Adjust salt and pepper to taste; serve.

Note: Cook each grain separately in salted water or vegetable broth according to package directions. To make enough for this recipe, we cooked ½ cup wild rice, 2/3 cup quick-cooking barley, ½ cup jasmine rice and 2/3 cup kamut (kah-MOOT), a large-grain wheat available in natural-food stores.

Each variety of wheat "berries" requires a different cooking time. To cook kamut: Toast 2/3 cup kamut in a dry skillet over medium-high heat, stirring constantly, until kernels pop and kamut develops a nutty fragrance. Rinse and drain; combine in a saucepan with 1½ cups water or vegetable stock and ½ teaspoon sea salt. Let stand at room temperature 1 hour. Bring to a boil; cook on high for 3 minutes. Reduce heat, cover and simmer until kernels are tender, about 1¼ hours, stirring occasionally and adding liquid as needed. If desired, add more salt to taste.

PER SERVING
calories 389 • fat 19.5g • % calories from fat 20 • saturated fat 3g • cholesterol 0 • protein 7g • carbohydrate 47g • sugar 2.5g • fiber 7.5g • sodium 231mg • calcium 28mg

CHOPPED VEGGIE SALAD

Yield: 8 servings (about 12 cups)

3 large tomatoes

2 medium onions, diced (about 1½ cups)

8 ounces good-quality Cheddar, diced into ¼-inch cubes

1 (14-ounce) can hearts of palm, drained

16 ounces marinated artichoke hearts, drained

½ cup shelled whole pistachio nuts, plus ¼ cup chopped pistachios for garnish

½ cup dried cranberries

½ cup raisins

¼ cup balsamic vinegar

½ cup olive oil

Salt

Ground black pepper

1½ heads butter lettuce, chopped (see note)

1 to 3 cups fresh or canned lump crab meat, optional

Cut tomatoes in half (across the "equator"); hold over the sink and squeeze gently to remove excess liquid. Chop into ½-inch pieces. (You should have about 5 cups.)

Combine tomatoes, onions and Cheddar in a large bowl. Slice hearts of palm in half lengthwise, then chop and add to the bowl. Chop artichoke hearts coarsely; add to the bowl. Add whole pistachios, cranberries and raisins; toss to combine.

Whisk together balsamic vinegar and olive oil; add to the bowl and toss well. Add salt and pepper to taste. Just before serving, divide lettuce among individual plates. Arrange about 1½ cups of the tomato mixture over lettuce on each plate. Sprinkle each salad with ½ tablespoon chopped pistachios. Top with crab meat, if desired.

Note: "Butter" lettuce means the loose-head varieties, such as Boston or bibb. Its soft texture requires gentle handling.

PER SERVING
calories 466 • fat 32g • % calories from fat 62 • saturated fat 8g • cholesterol 30mg • protein 14g • carbohydrate 33g • sugar 12g • fiber 6.5g • sodium 616mg • calcium 267mg • potassium 558mg

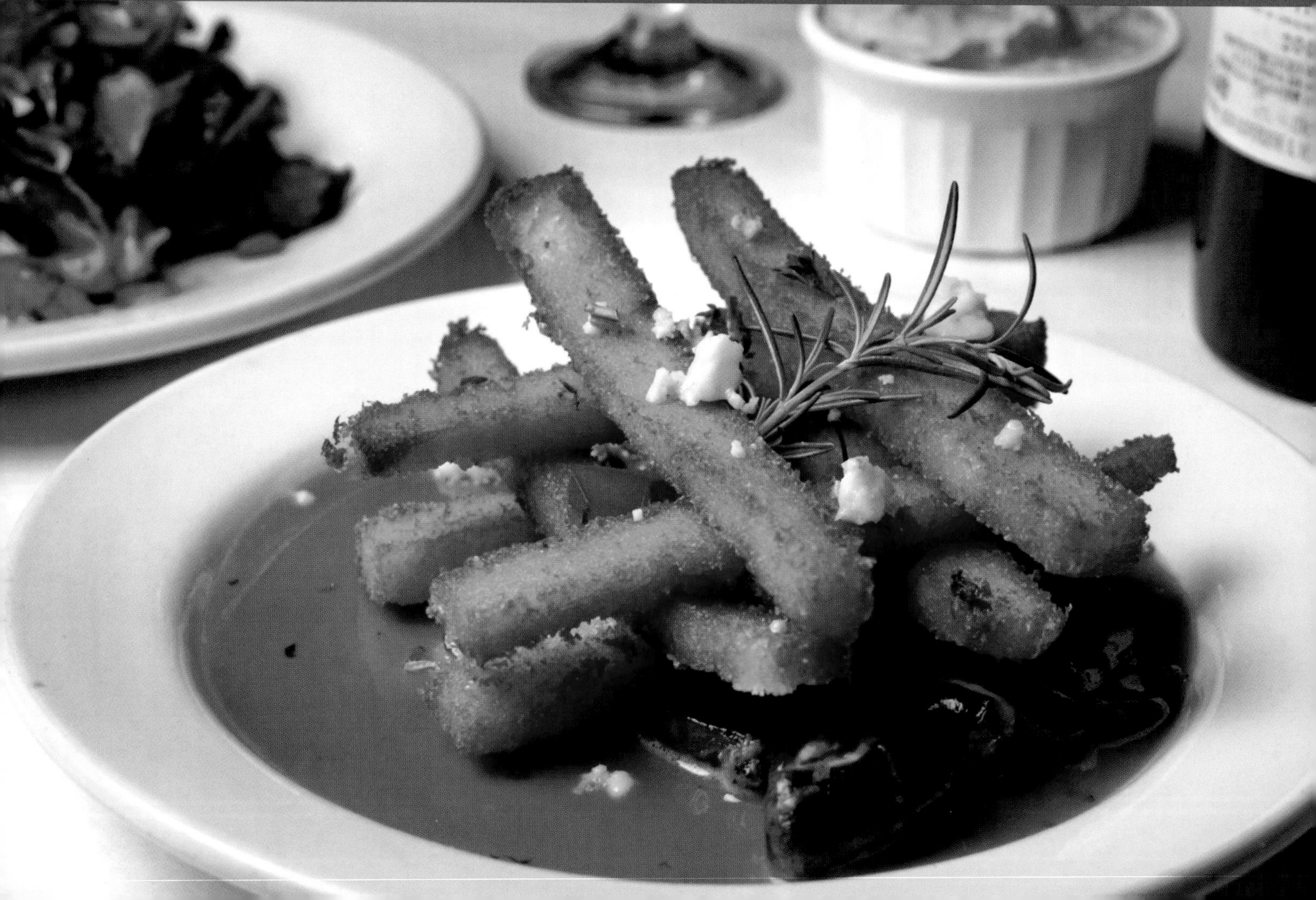

POLENTA FRIES

Yield: 8 servings

1½ cups chicken broth or water

1½ cups heavy cream

¼ teaspoon salt

1⅓ cups instant polenta (see tester's note)

2 tablespoons grated Parmesan cheese

Vegetable oil, for deep-frying

Marsala Gorgonzola Cream Sauce (see recipe) or marinara sauce

1 tablespoon diced tomato, for garnish

Combine chicken broth, cream and salt in a pot; bring to a boil. Add polenta. Stir with a wooden spoon until polenta pulls away from the sides of the pot, 2 to 3 minutes. Stir in Parmesan.

Spread polenta evenly about ½ inch thick on a greased sheet pan; chill. Slice into sticks about ½ inch wide and 4 inches long.

Heat oil in a deep-fryer to 350 degrees. Fry sticks until golden brown and crisp, 3 to 4 minutes; drain on paper towels. Serve with marinara sauce or Marsala Gorgonzola Cream Sauce. Garnish with tomato.

Tester's note: Yellow corn meal has a finer texture than instant polenta but may be substituted. If using meal, whisk into boiling liquid very gradually, as meal tends to clump. Polenta may be found in Italian markets and some supermarkets.

MARSALA GORGONZOLA CREAM SAUCE

Yield: 1⅓ cups

2 cups assorted sliced mushrooms (mixture of shiitake, oyster, crimini or your choice)

1 to 2 tablespoons extra-virgin olive oil

1⅔ cups sweet Marsala wine

1 cup heavy cream

¼ teaspoon minced garlic

1 small sprig fresh rosemary

½ teaspoon granulated sugar

¼ cup crumbled imported gorgonzola cheese, plus extra for garnish

1½ tablespoons butter

Sauté mushrooms in olive oil until tender; set aside.

Bring Marsala to a boil in a medium saucepan over medium heat; cook until liquid reduces to a syruplike consistency. (You should have about ⅓ cup.)

In another saucepan, bring cream to a boil; cook until reduced by half. Combine both reductions in one skillet. Stir in garlic, rosemary, sugar and cheese. Cook 4 to 5 minutes over medium heat until cheese melts. Add butter and mushrooms; stir until butter melts.

FRIES PER SERVING (without sauce)

calories 405 • fat 27.5g • % calories from fat 61 • saturated fat 15g • cholesterol 83mg • protein 6.5g • carbohydrate 34g • sugar 2g • fiber 3.5g • sodium 345mg • calcium 64mg

SAUCE PER (3-TABLESPOON) SERVING

calories 154 • fat 12g • % calories from fat 70 • saturated fat 6.5g • cholesterol 34mg • protein 2g • carbohydrate 4.5g • sugar 4g • fiber 0.5g • sodium 64mg • calcium 36mg

GERMAN POTATO PANCAKES

Yield: 4 servings (8 pancakes)

1 small onion, peeled and cut into chunks

1 large russet potato, peeled and cut into 1/2-inch pieces

4 eggs

7 tablespoons all-purpose flour

1/8 teaspoon salt

1 pinch ground black pepper

Vegetable oil, for frying

Combine onion, potato, eggs, flour, salt and pepper in a blender. Blend on high speed for 1 minute or until smooth.

Coat a frying pan with a thin layer of vegetable oil; place over medium-high heat. Ladle potato mixture, about 1/3 cup at a time, onto hot pan. Cook until bottoms of pancakes are lightly browned, then flip and cook other sides until browned.

PER SERVING
calories 244 • fat 14g • % calories from fat 52 • saturated fat 3g • cholesterol 212mg • protein 8.5g • carbohydrate 21g • sugar 1.5g • fiber 1.5g • sodium 147mg • calcium 36mg • potassium 243mg

CHEF HAYDEN'S CARROT SOUFFLÉ

Yield: 12 servings

10 ounces carrots (about 4 large)

5 tablespoons butter, plus more to prepare baking dishes

1/2 cup minus 1 tablespoon all-purpose flour

1 1/2 cups milk

1/2 teaspoon salt

1/4 teaspoon ground black pepper or to taste

1/2 teaspoon ground coriander

10 eggs, separated, at room temperature

Peel and coarsely chop carrots. Place in a saucepan, cover with water and cook until tender; drain. Place carrots in food processor; purée.

Preheat oven to 400 degrees. Generously butter two 1/2-quart soufflé dishes or straight-sided casseroles.

In a heavy saucepan over medium heat, combine butter, flour, milk, carrot purée, salt, pepper and coriander; bring to a simmer, stirring constantly. Cook and stir until thickened to a pastelike consistency, 5 to 10 minutes. Remove from heat. Whisk egg yolks; whisk some of the hot carrot mixture into the yolks to warm them, then gradually add the yolks to the mixture remaining in the pan.

Beat egg whites to stiff peaks; fold into carrot mixture in 3 additions. Gently transfer carrot mixture to the prepared baking dishes, filling them no more than 3/4 full. Bake about 25 minutes, until lightly browned and set in the center. Serve immediately.

PER SERVING
calories 169 • fat 11.5g • % calories from fat 61 • saturated fat 5.5g • cholesterol 233mg • protein 8g • carbohydrate 9.5g • sugar 5g • fiber 1g • sodium 212mg • calcium 76mg

SOUTHERN CREAM SPINACH

Yield: 8 generous servings

2 pounds frozen spinach

¼ cup (½ stick) butter

½ cup diced white onion

½ teaspoon minced garlic

5 tablespoons all-purpose flour

1⅓ cups half-and-half

¾ cup plus 2 tablespoons heavy cream

1 tablespoon plus 1 teaspoon granulated sugar

1 teaspoon salt

½ teaspoon ground black pepper

½ teaspoon garlic powder

Nonstick cooking spray

Garlic bread crumbs (see note)

Preheat oven to 350 degrees.

Bring a large pan of water to a boil. Add spinach, stir just until soft, then drain in a colander. Press spinach occasionally to remove excess liquid, but do not squeeze dry.

In a soup pot or Dutch oven, melt butter. Add onion and garlic; sauté over medium heat until just beginning to brown. Stir in flour; cook 2 to 3 minutes, stirring frequently, until flour is golden brown. Add half-and-half and cream; mix well. Cook until thickened, about 5 minutes, stirring frequently. Stir in sugar, salt, pepper and garlic powder. Stir in drained spinach; remove from heat.

Coat a 7-by-10-inch baking pan with cooking spray; add spinach mixture. Bake about 20 minutes, then top with bread crumbs and bake about 20 minutes more, until sides begin to brown.

Note: At Lotawata Creek, garlic bread crumbs are a byproduct of the housemade garlic croutons. Home cooks can crumble a few slices of dry white bread, toss with melted butter, toast in the oven at 325 degrees until golden brown, then sprinkle with garlic powder.

FARMHOUSE BREAD

Yield: 16 small loaves

5 tablespoons active dry yeast

2 cups warm water (100 to 115 degrees)

6¹⁄₃ cups bread flour, divided

2 cups medium-grind cracked wheat (available in natural-food stores)

2 tablespoons salt (see note)

3 tablespoons granulated sugar

3 tablespoons brown sugar

2 eggs

¹⁄₄ cup vegetable oil

Stir yeast into warm water; let stand until foamy, about 5 minutes.

In a large bowl of an electric mixer fitted with a dough hook, combine yeast mixture and 2½ cups flour. Mix at low speed about 2 minutes. Increase speed to medium; beat about 4 minutes.

Reduce speed to low. Beat in cracked wheat, salt, granulated sugar and brown sugar; mix about 3 minutes. Add eggs and oil. Gradually add enough of the remaining flour to make a soft dough; machine-knead about 5 minutes.

Use part of the remaining flour to generously coat a bread board; place dough on floured board. Knead by hand until dough resists pressure. (At this point, the dough may be tightly covered and refrigerated for future use. Remove from refrigerator, then proceed as directed.)

Divide dough into 16 equal pieces, about 4 ounces each. Shape into round balls; arrange on parchment-lined baking pans, allowing at least 2 inches between balls. Cover dough and pans completely with domed lids; allow to rise in a warm, moist place just until doubled, about 1 hour.

Preheat oven to 375 degrees. Bake until golden brown, about 20 minutes.

Note: We found this bread a little salty. Salt may be adjusted to taste.

PER LOAF

calories 317 • fat 5g • % calories from fat 14 • saturated fat 1g • cholesterol 27mg • protein 11g • carbohydrate 57g • sugar 6g • fiber 4g • sodium 894mg • calcium 22mg • potassium 207mg

SOUR CREAM BLUEBERRY BREAD

Yield: 2 loaves (about 16 servings)

1½ cups plus 1 tablespoon unbleached all-purpose flour, divided

1 tablespoon baking powder

½ teaspoon salt

6 tablespoons (¾ stick) unsalted butter or margarine, softened

1¼ cups granulated sugar

2 eggs

1 teaspoon vanilla

½ cup sour cream

1½ cups frozen blueberries (do not thaw)

½ cup coarsely chopped walnuts, divided

Grease and flour two 7½-by-3½-inch metal loaf pans. Preheat the oven to 375 degrees.

In a small bowl, combine 1½ cups flour, baking powder and salt; set aside.

Using an electric mixer, beat butter with sugar in a large bowl until light. Add eggs, vanilla and sour cream; beat well. Blend in flour mixture; beat on medium-high speed for 1 minute.

In a separate bowl, lightly toss blueberries with remaining 1 tablespoon flour. Carefully fold blueberries into batter.

Set prepared pans on a larger baking sheet for easy handling; divide batter evenly between the pans. Sprinkle each loaf with ¼ cup walnuts. Bake loaves about 45 minutes, until they are light golden brown and the center springs up when pushed lightly. Let cool completely on a wire rack.

Note: To make muffins, grease and flour 12 medium muffin cups. Divide batter among cups. Bake about 25 minutes, until muffins are golden brown and spring back when touched in the center. Let cool on a wire rack.

PER SERVING

calories 197 • fat 9g • % calories from fat 41 • saturated fat 4g • cholesterol 42mg • protein 3g • carbohydrate 26.5g • sugar 16.5g • fiber 1g • sodium 161mg • calcium 61mg • potassium 48mg

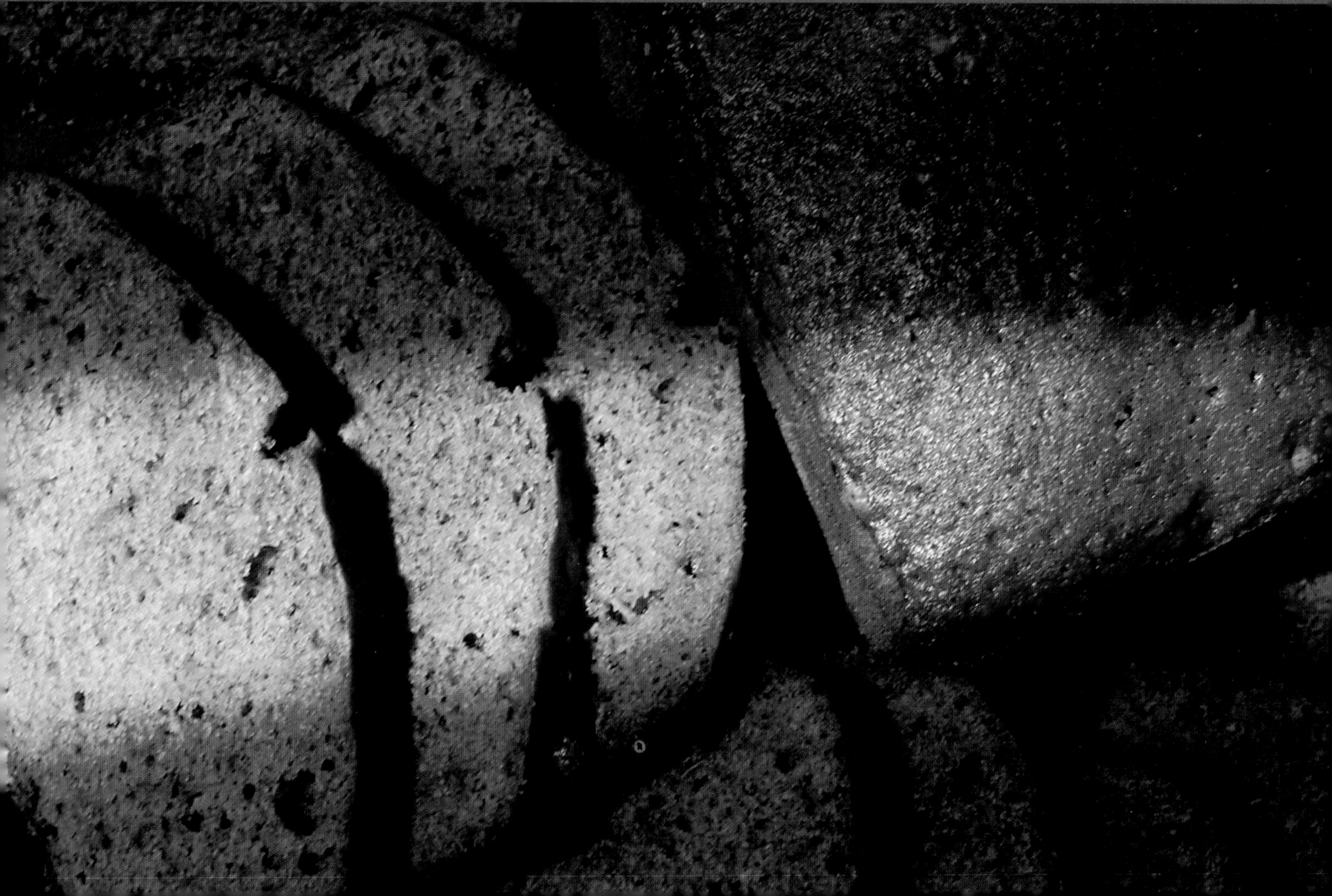

ZUCCHINI BREAD

Yield: 2 loaves (16 servings)

3 eggs

1 cup vegetable oil

2 cups granulated sugar

2 teaspoons vanilla

2 cups grated zucchini (about 2 small zucchini)

3 cups all-purpose flour

1/2 teaspoon baking soda

1/2 teaspoon baking powder

2 tablespoons ground cinnamon

1/2 cup chopped pecans

Grease and flour two 9-by-5-inch or 8-by-4-inch loaf pans. Preheat the oven to 350 degrees.

In a large bowl, combine eggs, oil, sugar and vanilla; beat with a fork or a whisk until smooth. Stir in zucchini until well blended; set aside.

In a medium bowl, stir together flour, baking soda, baking powder and cinnamon until thoroughly combined. Add to egg mixture, 1 cup at a time. Beat until blended. Stir in pecans.

Pour batter into prepared pans. Bake about 50 minutes or until a wooden pick inserted in the center comes out clean. Let cool 10 minutes, then remove from pans. Cooled loaves may be frozen.

Note: Batter also can be baked in two 8-inch-square pans for 35 to 40 minutes or until done.

PER SERVING
calories 350 • fat 17.5g • % calories from fat 45 • saturated fat 2.5g • cholesterol 40mg • protein 4g • carbohydrate 45g • sugar 25g • fiber 1.5g • sodium 65mg • calcium 28mg • potassium 89mg

DESSERTS

Green Apple Cobblers with Sauce of the Missouri River Valley • Apple Crisp • Pineapple-Coconut Pie • Praline Custard Pie • Buttermilk Pie • Chocolate Pecan Pie • Chocolate-Chip Pie • Bailey's Cheesecake • Snickers Cheesecake • Crème Custard Napoleon • Brioche Bread Pudding • Double Chocolate Bread Pudding • Truffle Cookies • Chocolate-Dipped Hazelnut Biscotti • Kheer • Chocolate Chunk Muffins • Orange Fluff Cake • Sticky Toffee Pudding • Dark Chocolate Torte

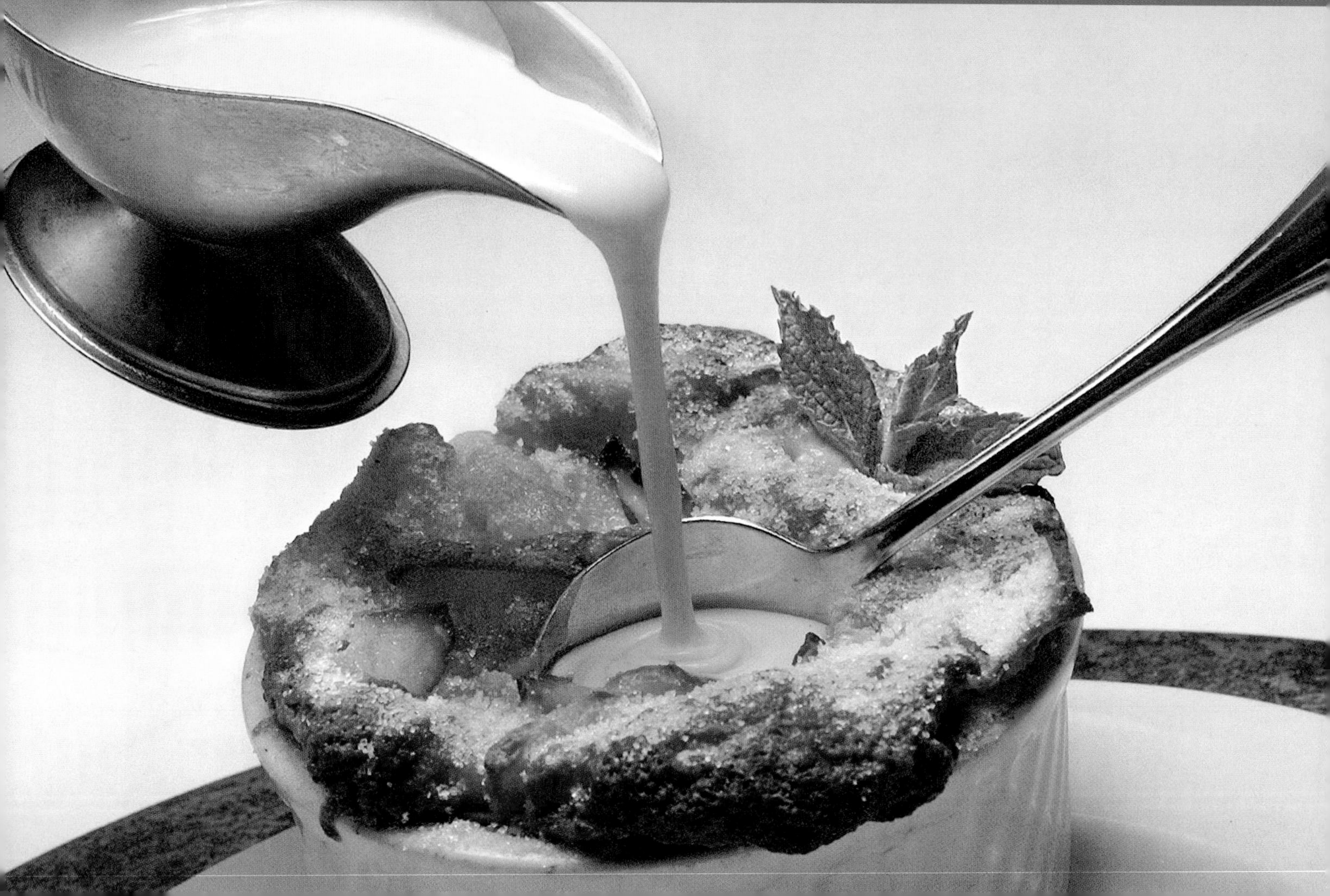

GREEN APPLE COBBLERS WITH SAUCE OF THE MISSOURI RIVER VALLEY

Yield: 6 servings

FOR SAUCE:

1 cup semi-dry Missouri wine (such as Stone Hill Seyval)

1 cup heavy cream

2/3 cup granulated sugar

1 egg, beaten

2 egg yolks, beaten

FOR COBBLERS:

1 teaspoon butter

3/4 teaspoon plus 1 cup granulated sugar, divided

1 cup all-purpose flour

1 1/2 teaspoons baking powder

1/2 cup milk

2 eggs, lightly beaten

1 1/2 cups peeled, cored and thinly sliced Granny Smith apples

To prepare sauce: In a small pan over medium heat, simmer wine until reduced to slightly less than 1/4 cup; set aside.

Combine cream, sugar, whole egg and yolks in the top of a double boiler; cook over simmering water, stirring constantly, until mixture thickens and coats the back of a spoon. Stir in reduced wine. Cover and chill until cold. (Makes 1 1/2 cups sauce.)

To prepare cobblers: Preheat oven to 350 degrees. Butter 6 (6-ounce) ramekins or custard cups; dust with 3/4 teaspoon sugar.

In a medium bowl, combine flour, remaining 1 cup sugar and baking powder. Add milk and eggs; beat just until smooth. Do not overbeat.

Divide apple slices among ramekins; spoon batter over apples. (Ramekins should be about 3/4 full.) Bake 30 to 35 minutes, until a toothpick inserted in the center comes out clean. Serve hot cobblers with cold sauce.

PER SERVING
calories 447 • fat 14.5g • % calories from fat 29 • saturated fat 8g • cholesterol 180mg • protein 7g • carbohydrate 71g • sugar 53g • fiber 1g • sodium 174mg • calcium 130mg • potassium 136mg

APPLE CRISP

Yield: 6 large servings

FOR CRUST:

1 cup all-purpose flour

¼ teaspoon granulated sugar

⅓ cup solid vegetable shortening

3 to 4 tablespoons ice water

FOR CRUMB TOPPING:

½ cup granulated sugar

1 cup all-purpose flour

¼ teaspoon apple pie spice

¼ teaspoon ground cinnamon

⅛ teaspoon salt

⅓ cup soft margarine

FOR APPLE FILLING:

1 cup granulated sugar

½ cup all-purpose flour

1 teaspoon ground cinnamon

½ teaspoon apple pie spice

1 dash salt

¼ teaspoon powdered ascorbic acid (such as Fruit Fresh)

2½ pounds Jonathan or Jonagold apples, peeled and sliced about ¼ inch thick (about 8 cups)

1 teaspoon vanilla

2 teaspoons butter

To prepare crust: Sift flour into a medium bowl. Stir sugar into flour; cut in shortening with a pastry blender or two table knives. Gradually add ice water, stirring with a fork until a dough begins to form. Shape into a ball, cover with plastic wrap and refrigerate until cold.

Roll chilled dough to line the bottom and sides of a 9-inch-square, 2-inch-deep metal baking pan; trim top edge level with top of pan. Set aside.

Preheat oven to 350 degrees (convection oven to 325 degrees).

To prepare filling: In a large bowl, stir together sugar, flour, cinnamon, apple pie spice, salt and ascorbic acid. Toss apples with vanilla; add to dry ingredients, tossing well to combine. Pour apple mixture into prepared crust; dot with butter. (You should have enough apples to fill the pan to the top.)

To prepare topping: Stir sugar, flour, apple pie spice, cinnamon, salt and margarine together to make crumbs. Sprinkle about half the crumbs over the apples; shake the pan gently to "settle" the crumbs. Sprinkle on remaining crumbs.

Bake about 1 hour (convection oven, 45 minutes to 1 hour) or until apples are bubbly and topping is lightly browned. Let cool before serving.

PER SERVING
calories 675 • fat 23g • % calories from fat 31 • saturated fat 5g • cholesterol 3mg • protein 6g • carbohydrate 111g • sugar 67g • fiber 4g • sodium 157mg • calcium 25mg • potassium 209mg

PINEAPPLE-COCONUT PIE

Yield: 8 servings

FOR CRUST:

1 cup all-purpose flour

¹/₂ teaspoon salt

¹/₃ cup shortening

2 to 3¹/₂ tablespoons ice water

FOR FILLING:

3 eggs, beaten

1¹/₂ cups granulated sugar

¹/₄ teaspoon salt

2 tablespoons all-purpose flour

¹/₄ cup (¹/₂ stick) butter, melted

1 (8-ounce) can crushed pineapple

1 cup sweetened flaked coconut

To prepare crust: To measure flour, spoon lightly into a 1-cup dry measure. Level off. Sift flour and salt together into a large bowl. Cut in shortening with a pastry blender or two table knives until mixture forms particles slightly larger than grains of rice. Sprinkle with ice water, 1 tablespoon at a time. Toss gently with a fork until all particles are uniformly moistened and will barely stick together.

Shape mixture into a ball. Roll out on a lightly floured pastry cloth to form a circle. Ease into a 9-inch pie plate; flute the edges.

To prepare filling: Preheat oven to 400 degrees. In a large bowl, combine eggs, sugar, salt, flour, melted butter, pineapple and coconut. Mix well. Pour into pie shell.

Bake at 400 degrees for 15 minutes. Reduce temperature to 300 degrees; bake for 20 to 30 minutes or until center seems set and a knife inserted into the center comes out clean.

PER SERVING

calories 444 • fat 20g • % calories from fat 41 • saturated fat 10g • cholesterol 94mg • protein 5g • carbohydrate 61g • sugar 47g • fiber 1.5g • sodium 280mg • calcium 21mg • potassium 121mg

SOMETHING ELSAH was located in Plaza Frontenac in Frontenac, Mo.

PRALINE CUSTARD PIE

Yield: 8 servings

⅓ cup packed light brown sugar

½ cup chopped pecans

⅓ cup plus 1 tablespoon butter, divided

1 (9-inch) baked pie shell

1 cup granulated sugar

3 tablespoons cornstarch

⅛ teaspoon salt

3 egg yolks

2 cups milk

1 teaspoon vanilla

1½ cups whipped cream, plus more for optional garnish

Lightly toasted pecan pieces, for optional garnish

Preheat oven to 450 degrees.

In a small pan, heat brown sugar, pecans and ⅓ cup butter; cook and stir until butter is melted. Spread in baked pie shell; place in oven and bake 5 minutes. Let cool.

Combine granulated sugar and cornstarch in a medium saucepan. Beat in salt, egg yolks and milk. Cook over medium heat until very thick, stirring constantly. Add vanilla and remaining 1 tablespoon butter; cook and stir just until butter is melted. Measure out 1 cup custard; set aside. Pour remaining custard into prepared pie shell.

When the 1 cup of custard cools, fold in whipped cream. Spread on top of pie; chill. Garnish with toasted pecans, dollops of whipped cream or both.

BUTTERMILK PIE

Yield: 8 servings

2 cups granulated sugar

¼ cup (½ stick) butter, softened

3 eggs

¼ cup all-purpose flour

¼ teaspoon salt

1 cup buttermilk

½ teaspoon vanilla

1 unbaked 9-inch deep-dish pie shell

½ cup toasted pecan halves

Preheat oven to 300 degrees.

Beat sugar and butter until light and fluffy; beat in eggs, one at a time. Stir together flour and salt; gradually beat into the butter mixture. Beat in buttermilk and vanilla. Pour filling into pie shell. Sprinkle with pecans.

Bake in the lowest third of the oven for 75 minutes or until the custard is set and top is lightly browned. Let cool before slicing.

PER SERVING

Calories 434 • fat 18g • % calories from fat 37 • saturated fat 6.5g • cholesterol 96mg • protein 5g • carbohydrate 63g • sugar 52g • fiber 1g • sodium 237mg • calcium 56mg • potassium 124mg   189

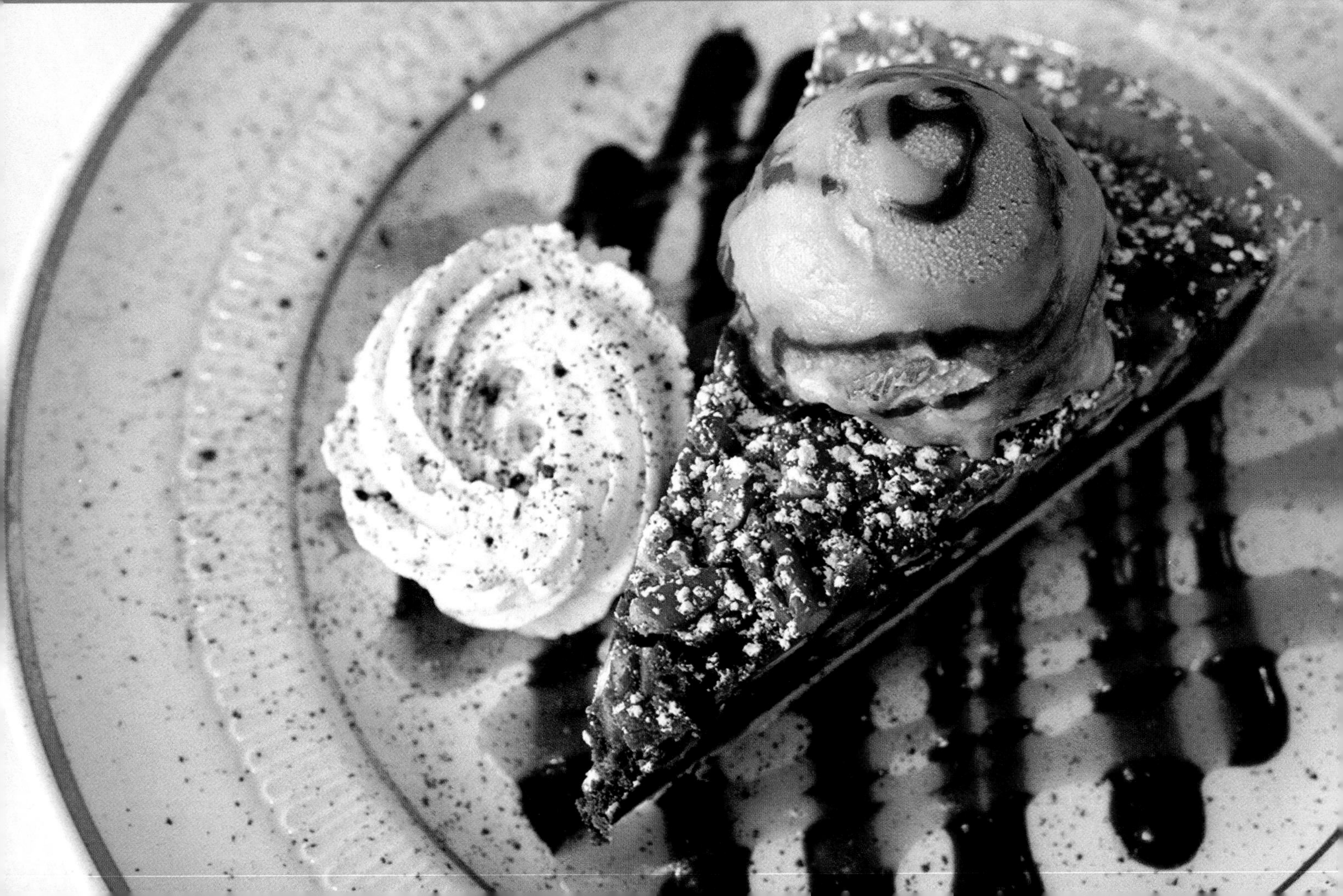

CHOCOLATE PECAN PIE

Yield: 8 servings

½ cup (1 stick) unsalted butter

1½ ounces bittersweet chocolate

2 eggs, beaten

2 tablespoons milk

1 tablespoon vanilla

1 cup packed brown sugar

½ cup granulated sugar

1 tablespoon all-purpose flour

1 unbaked 9-inch pie shell

1 cup pecan halves or large pieces

Cappuccino or coffee ice cream, for optional garnish

Chocolate sauce, for optional garnish

Caramel sauce, for optional garnish

Preheat oven to 325 degrees. Slowly melt butter and chocolate in the top of a double boiler placed over simmering water; do not let boil. Remove from heat.

In a small bowl, combine eggs, milk and vanilla. Beat until blended.

In another small bowl, combine sugars and flour; mix well. Add sugar mixture to melted chocolate and butter. Stir until blended. Add egg mixture slowly; mix well. Pour into pie shell. Top with pecans.

Bake pie for about 45 minutes or until center is set. Let pie cool on a wire rack. Serve topped with ice cream, chocolate and caramel sauces.

ER SERVING

alories 498 • fat 30g • % calories from fat 54 • saturated fat 10.5g • cholesterol 83mg • protein 4g • carbohydrate 53g • sugar 43g • fiber 2g • sodium 134mg • calcium 51mg • potassium 198mg

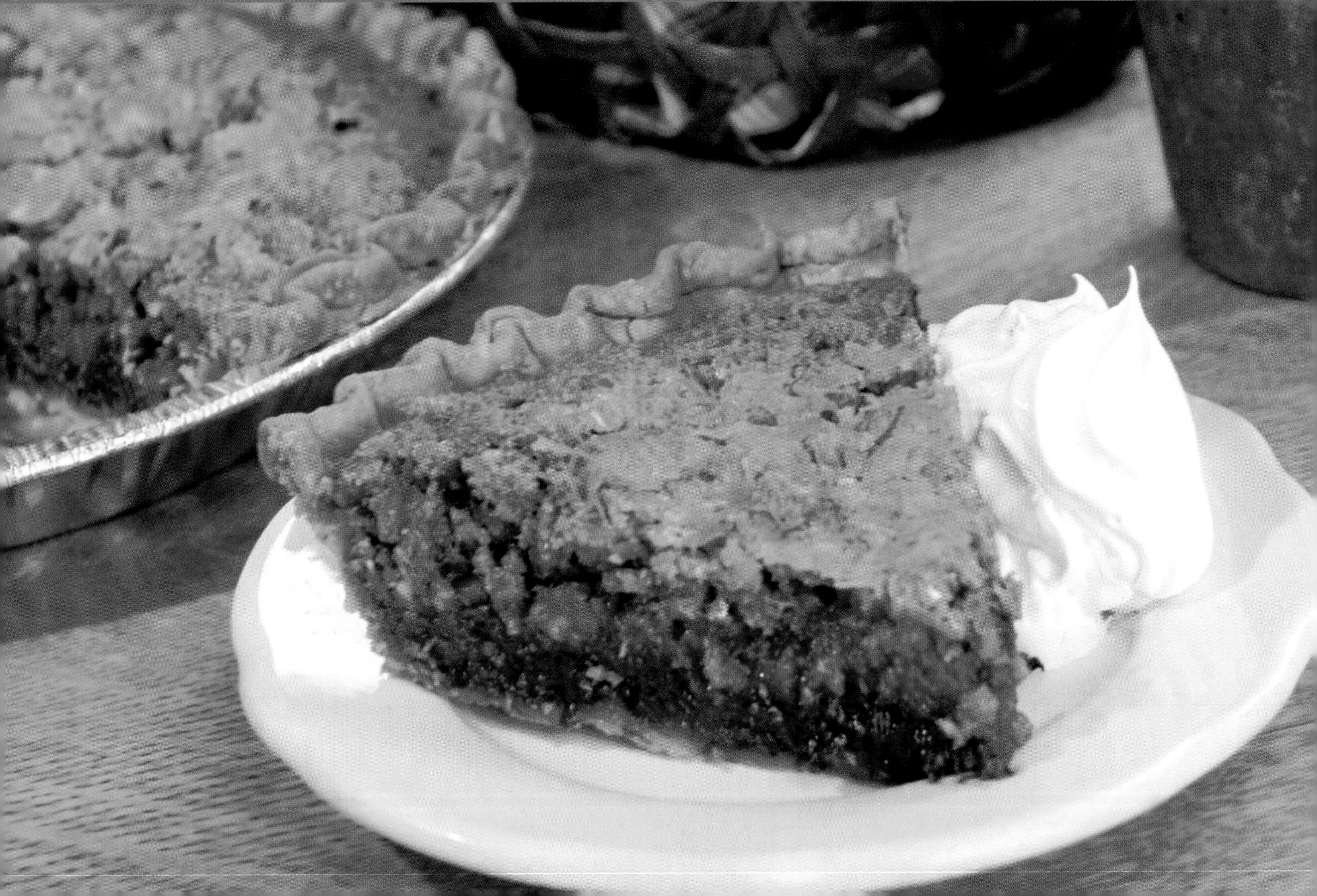

CHOCOLATE-CHIP PIE

Yield: 8 servings

Pastry for single-crust pie

³/₄ cup all-purpose flour

³/₄ cup granulated sugar

³/₄ cup packed brown sugar

**1 cup (2 sticks) butter,
   melted and cooled**

3 eggs

1¹/₂ cups chopped pecans

1¹/₂ cups chocolate chips

Preheat oven to 325 degrees. Line a 9- or 10-inch deep-dish pie plate with pastry; crimp edges.

In bowl of electric mixer, combine flour and sugars; mix well. Add cooled butter, and start beating at medium speed. Add eggs; beat until mixture is light and well combined, 2 to 3 minutes. Stir in nuts and chips by hand.

Pour filling into pie shell. Bake until crust is baked and top is golden, about 50 to 55 minutes. Let cool completely before slicing.

PER SERVING
calories 839 • fat 55g • % calories from fat 59 • saturated fat 23g • cholesterol 140mg • protein 7.5g • carbohydrate 78.5g • sugar 58g • fiber 4.5g • sodium 143mg • calcium 65mg • potassium 340mg

BAILEY'S CHEESECAKE

Yield: 16 servings

FOR CHEESECAKE:

1 cup plus 2 tablespoons chocolate cookie crumbs

2 ½ tablespoons melted butter

3 (8-ounce) packages cream cheese, softened

1 cup granulated sugar

1 teaspoon almond extract

½ teaspoon vanilla

2 eggs

FOR BAILEY'S SAUCE:

½ cup white or semisweet chocolate chips

1 cup Bailey's Irish Cream liqueur

To prepare cheesecake: Preheat oven to 300 degrees. Butter the bottom of a 9-inch springform pan.

Mix cookie crumbs and melted butter until thoroughly blended; spread in bottom of pan.

Blend cream cheese, sugar, almond extract and vanilla. Add eggs 1 at a time. Spread cream cheese mixture over crumb crust. Bake about 55 minutes, until just set in center.

To prepare sauce: Heat chocolate and Bailey's in the top of a double boiler set over simmering water until smooth. Let cook until sauce reaches desired texture.

To serve, drizzle sauce over slices of cheesecake.

PER SERVING
calories 340 • fat 22.5g • % calories from fat 60 • saturated fat 13.5g • cholesterol 89mg • protein 5g • carbohydrate 26g • sugar 21g • fiber 0 • sodium 200mg • calcium 50mg • potassium 81mg

SNICKERS CHEESECAKE

Yield: 14 servings

FOR CRUST:

1½ cups graham cracker crumbs

6 tablespoons (¾ stick) butter, melted

FOR BROWNIE LAYER:

¾ cup all-purpose flour

1 teaspoon baking powder

¼ teaspoon salt

1 cup (2 sticks) butter

8 ounces semisweet chocolate chips

2 ounces unsweetened chocolate, coarsely chopped

2 whole eggs

2 egg yolks

1 cup granulated sugar

2 teaspoons vanilla

4 Snickers bars (regular size), cut into bite-size chunks

FOR CHEESECAKE LAYER:

3 (8-ounce) packages cream cheese

¾ cup granulated sugar

3 eggs

2 teaspoons vanilla

FOR GANACHE:

½ cup heavy cream

2 tablespoons (¼ stick) unsalted butter

½ cup semisweet chocolate chips

1 tablespoon Bailey's Irish Cream or other liqueur, such as Kahlua or Grand Marnier, optional

To prepare crust: Preheat oven to 350 degrees. In a medium bowl, stir together graham cracker crumbs and melted butter. Press into the bottom of a 10-inch springform pan.

To prepare brownie layer: Sift together flour, baking powder and salt. Set aside.

In the top of a double boiler, melt butter, chocolate chips and unsweetened chocolate, stirring occasionally. Set aside.

In the large bowl of an electric mixer, beat together eggs and yolks on high speed. Beat in sugar, then vanilla until blended. Reduce mixer speed to medium-low. Alternate adding the flour mixture and melted chocolate, a little at a time, beginning and ending with flour. Mix just until flour is incorporated. Do not overbeat. Pour over crust.

Bake for 16 minutes. Remove from oven. Let cool 10 minutes. Push cut-up Snickers bars into brownie layer. Reduce oven heat to 325 degrees.

While brownie layer is cooling, prepare cheesecake layer: In a large, clean bowl of an electric mixer, combine cream cheese and sugar. Beat with clean beaters until well-blended. Add eggs, one at a time, beating well. Beat in vanilla. Pour cheesecake layer over brownie layer.

Return pan to oven. Bake for about 45 minutes or until the sides begin to pull away from the pan and the top layer begins to look firm. The middle may be soft, but it should not be runny.

Let cake cool for 1 hour, then refrigerate for at least 4 hours before removing the sides of the springform pan.

To prepare ganache: Bring cream and butter to a boil in a medium saucepan. Remove from heat. Stir in chocolate chips. Whisk until smooth. (Or place hot cream mixture and chocolate chips in a food processor and process until smooth.) Stir in liqueur. Let cool.

Spoon cooled ganache into a pastry bag. Pipe decoratively onto finished cake.

PER SERVING
calories 797 • fat 55.5g • % calories from fat 63 • saturated fat 33g • cholesterol 224mg • protein 10.5g • carbohydrate 64g • sugar 48.5g • fiber 3g • sodium 351mg • calcium 112mg • potassium 285mg

197

CRÈME CUSTARD NAPOLEON

Yield: 8 servings

FOR CRÈME
CUSTARD:

**2½ cups heavy
cream**

**1 tablespoon
vanilla**

10 egg yolks

**1 cup granulated
sugar**

FOR PHYLLO CRISP:

**6 sheets phyllo
dough, thawed**

**5 tablespoons
unsalted butter,
melted**

**1½ cups
powdered sugar,
divided**

FOR CARAMEL
SAUCE:

**1 cup granulated
sugar**

**¼ cup plus 2
tablespoons
water**

**¼ cup heavy
cream**

**¼ cup (½ stick)
unsalted butter,
cut into cubes**

FOR ASSEMBLY:

**4 bananas, sliced
about ¾ inch
thick**

**Powdered sugar,
for garnish**

**Whipped cream,
for garnish**

**Shaved chocolate,
for garnish**

To prepare crème custard: In a saucepan with a heavy bottom, heat cream and vanilla just until bubbles begin to form around the edge of the pan; remove from heat. In a mixing bowl, beat egg yolks and sugar with an electric mixer at high speed until very pale and the mixture forms a thick ribbon when beaters are lifted, 4 to 5 minutes. Gradually whisk cream into yolk mixture. Cover with plastic wrap pressed directly on the surface; refrigerate about 1 hour to cool.

Preheat the oven to 350 degrees. Pour custard into a 7-by-11-inch baking pan. Place in a larger pan, then add water to the larger pan to a depth of about ½ inch. Bake custard until it reaches a gelatinlike consistency, about 1 hour. Chill until firm or up to 3 days.

To prepare phyllo crisp: Preheat the oven to 350 degrees. Line a large baking sheet with parchment paper.

Place a sheet of phyllo on the baking sheet; brush phyllo with melted butter. Using a flour sifter, sprinkle with about ¼ cup powdered sugar. Repeat layers with remaining 5 sheets phyllo, melted butter and powdered sugar.

Cover the stack with parchment paper, then place a second baking sheet on top to keep the phyllo flat. Bake 10 to 12 minutes. Turn the baking sheets (with phyllo stack between) upside down; bake 5 minutes more or until phyllo is light golden brown. Cut into 16 equal pieces and let cool.

To prepare caramel sauce: In a saucepan with a heavy bottom, stir sugar into water until dissolved; place over medium-high heat and bring to a boil without stirring. Cook until sugar-water turns amber in color, watching carefully. Remove from heat. Slowly and carefully whisk in cream. (Mixture will sputter and foam.) Whisk in butter.

To assemble Napoleons: Combine caramel sauce and sliced bananas in a sauté pan. Place over medium heat until warm. Cut custard into 16 pieces; place one piece on a chilled plate and top with a phyllo crisp. Repeat layers. Spoon caramel-banana mixture around each Napoleon, dividing evenly. Garnish with a sprinkling of powdered sugar, a dollop of whipped cream and a few shavings of chocolate.

PER SERVING
calories 858 • fat 49.5g • % calories from fat 52 • saturated fat 29g • cholesterol 402mg • protein 6.5g • carbohydrate 96.5g • sugar 79.5g • fiber 2g • sodium 113mg • calcium 89mg • potassium 313mg

HARVEST 1059 South Big Bend Boulevard • Richmond Heights, Mo. • 314-645-3522 • www.harveststlouis.com

BRIOCHE BREAD PUDDING

Yield: 10 servings

Butter, to prepare baking dish

2 loaves or 1 pound brioche, to make 8 cups cubes

2 cups milk

2 cups heavy cream

³/₄ cup granulated sugar

¹/₄ teaspoon vanilla

¹/₂ vanilla bean, split

¹/₂ cinnamon stick

¹/₄ teaspoon freshly grated nutmeg

3 egg yolks

3 whole eggs

Bourbon Currant Sauce (see recipe)

Unsweetened whipped cream, flavored with vanilla

Butter a 2½- to 3-quart baking dish. Preheat oven to 350 degrees.

Remove crust from brioche. Cut brioche into 1-inch cubes. Place in a large bowl. In a saucepan, combine milk, cream, sugar, vanilla, vanilla bean, cinnamon stick and nutmeg. Slowly bring liquid to about 120 degrees, until it is just warm to the touch. Quickly whisk in egg yolks and whole eggs; continue whisking until mixture is slightly thickened or coats a metal spoon. Keep heat low; do not let boil or eggs will scramble and custard will not form.

Let custard cool slightly. Remove cinnamon stick and vanilla bean. Slowly pour custard over cubed brioche. Toss, then transfer to baking dish. Bake about 20 to 25 minutes, until top is lightly browned. Serve warm with Bourbon Currant Sauce and vanilla-flavored whipped cream.

BOURBON CURRANT SAUCE

Yield: 3 cups

2 cups granulated sugar

¹/₂ teaspoon baking soda

¹/₂ teaspoon vanilla

2 tablespoons light corn syrup

1 cup buttermilk

1 cup (2 sticks) unsalted butter

¹/₂ cup bourbon

¹/₂ cup dried currants

Combine sugar, baking soda, vanilla, corn syrup, buttermilk and butter in a large saucepan; bring to a boil. Reduce heat and simmer until mixture begins to darken, about 20 minutes. Remove from heat; stir in bourbon and currants. Serve warm.

BRIOCHE BREAD PUDDING PER SERVING (without Bourbon Currant Sauce)
calories 482 • fat 32g • % calories from fat 60 • saturated fat 19g • cholesterol 262mg • protein 9.5g • carbohydrate 39g • sugar 17g • fiber 0.5g • sodium 349mg • calcium 117mg • potassium 132mg

BOURBON CURRANT SAUCE PER ¹/₄-CUP SERVING
calories 324 • fat 15g • % calories from fat 42 • saturated fat 10g • cholesterol 41mg • protein 1g • carbohydrate 41g • sugar 39g • fiber 0.5g • sodium 79mg • calcium 34mg • potassium 90mg

DOUBLE CHOCOLATE BREAD PUDDING

Yield: 15 servings

10 cups (3/4-inch) bread cubes
1 cup (2 sticks) butter, melted
3 1/2 cups milk
1 1/2 cups granulated sugar
11 whole eggs
4 egg yolks
1 1/2 teaspoons vanilla
10 1/2 ounces dark chocolate
4 1/2 ounces white chocolate
1/4 cup packed brown sugar
Whiskey Sauce (see recipe)
Whipped cream

Preheat oven to 350 degrees. Toss bread cubes with melted butter, place on a sheet pan and toast in oven for 15 minutes or until golden. Transfer to a large bowl to cool completely.

Whisk together milk, granulated sugar, whole eggs, yolks and vanilla. Pour over cooled bread cubes; mix well. Refrigerate for 30 minutes.

Return the oven to 350 degrees. Shave chocolates into thin pieces; toss with brown sugar. Add chocolate mixture to soaked bread cubes; mix well. Place in a buttered 9-by-13-inch baking pan or casserole that is at least 2 inches deep; cover tightly with foil.

Place in a larger pan. Add enough hot water to the larger pan to reach halfway up the sides of the smaller pan. Bake for 1 hour or until custard is just set.

To serve, spoon warm bread pudding into small bowls, drizzle with Whiskey Sauce and top with whipped cream.

WHISKEY SAUCE

Yield: 2 1/2 cups

3/4 teaspoon cornstarch
2 tablespoons water
3/4 cup bourbon
3/4 cup granulated sugar
1 1/2 cups heavy cream
3/4 teaspoon vanilla

Stir together cornstarch and water; set aside. Combine bourbon, sugar and cream in a saucepan. Bring to a simmer over medium heat, stirring just until sugar is dissolved. When mixture comes to a simmer, stir in cornstarch mixture in a slow, steady stream. Cook, stirring, until sauce returns to a simmer; remove from heat and stir in vanilla.

PUDDING PER SERVING (without whiskey sauce or whipped cream)
Calories 508 • fat 33g • % calories from fat 58 • saturated fat 18g • cholesterol 254mg • protein 11.5g • carbohydrate 49.5g • sugar 33g • fiber 3.5g • sodium 217mg • calcium 154mg

SAUCE PER (2-TABLESPOON) SERVING
Calories 112 • fat 6.5g • % calories from fat 52 • saturated fat 4g • cholesterol 24mg • protein 0.5g • carbohydrate 8g • sugar 8g • fiber 0 • sodium 7mg • calcium 12mg

TRUFFLE COOKIES

Yield: about 50 cookies

FOR COOKIE DOUGH:

¾ cup (1½ sticks) unsalted butter, softened

½ cup granulated sugar

1 egg

⅛ teaspoon salt

Seeds from 1 small vanilla bean

2¼ cups all-purpose flour

FOR TRUFFLE FILLING:

½ cup heavy cream

1 tablespoon butter

1 tablespoon granulated sugar

9 ounces milk chocolate, chopped

1 teaspoon Grand Marnier or another liqueur

FOR TOPPING:

10 ounces milk chocolate, finely chopped

Finely chopped roasted almonds or hazelnuts or semisweet chocolate, melted

To prepare dough: In the large bowl of an electric mixer, beat butter and sugar until light. Add egg and salt; scrape bowl, then beat until blended. Gradually beat in vanilla seeds, then beat in flour in three additions. Refrigerate dough until firm, about 1 hour.

Preheat oven to 350 degrees. Knead dough 3 or 4 turns, until smooth. Roll out to ⅛ inch thick on a lightly floured board. Using a 1¼-inch round or fluted cookie cutter (or another shape of your choice), cut out 50 circles. Arrange on a lightly greased cookie sheet; bake until lightly browned, about 12 minutes. Let cool.

To prepare truffle filling: In a small pot, combine cream, butter and sugar; stir over medium heat until sugar has dissolved. Bring to a boil. Remove from heat; add chocolate and liqueur, and whisk until smooth. Chill about 45 minutes, stirring every 10 minutes, until slightly firm.

Using an electric mixer with a whisk-style beater, whip truffle mixture until light and creamy, about 1½ minutes.

If filling is too firm to pipe, warm slightly and rewhip. If filling is too soft, refrigerate and rewhip. Use a pastry bag fitted with a ½-inch round tip to pipe a mound of truffle filling onto each cookie. The bottom of the mound should reach almost to the edges of the cookie, tapering slightly until it reaches about ¾ inch tall. Refrigerate until firm.

To prepare topping: Warm milk chocolate in a double boiler or on low power in the microwave until chocolate can be stirred smooth. (Chocolate should be melted, but not too warm.) Holding cookies carefully, dip the tops in chocolate to cover the truffle filling. Place on parchment-lined cookie sheets.

If desired, sprinkle with nuts before chocolate sets, then chill. Alternately, chill cookies, then drizzle with semisweet chocolate. Refrigerate in a well-sealed container; cookies keep well for 10 days.

PER COOKIE
calories 125 • fat 7.5g • % calories from fat 54 • saturated fat 4.5g • cholesterol 18mg • protein 1g • carbohydrate 13.5g • sugar 8.5g • fiber 0.5g • sodium 9mg • calcium 6mg • potassium 47mg

205

CHOCOLATE-DIPPED HAZELNUT BISCOTTI

Yield: About 8 dozen

2 cups hazelnuts

1 cup (2 sticks) unsalted butter, slightly softened

1½ cups granulated sugar

4 extra-large eggs

2 tablespoons orange liqueur

2 tablespoons grated orange zest (colored portion of peel)

3¼ cups sifted all-purpose flour (sift before measuring)

4½ teaspoons baking powder

2 tablespoons crushed coriander seeds

24 ounces semisweet chocolate, melted (see note)

Day one: Preheat the oven to 325 degrees. Spread hazelnuts on a baking sheet; bake about 25 minutes, tossing once. (When toasted, the nuts will be golden brown under the skins.) Let cool, then rub handfuls of nuts between your palms to remove the skins. Chop hazelnuts coarsely; set aside.

Beat butter until very light; add sugar gradually. Add eggs, one at a time. Mix in liqueur and orange zest. In a small bowl, combine flour and baking powder. Add flour mixture to butter mixture, a cup at a time, until well blended. Stir in hazelnuts and coriander seeds.

Line a 9-by-13-inch baking pan with a sheet of plastic wrap about twice as long as the pan. Pack the dough into the pan. Cover the top of the dough completely with plastic wrap. Place another 9-by-13-inch pan on top of the dough; weigh down the top pan (a six-pack of soda cans works well). Chill the dough overnight.

Day two: Preheat the oven to 350 degrees. Remove the plastic wrap; transfer the dough to a floured board. Cut the dough into 5 equal strips, each 9 inches long. With floured hands, roll each strip into a cylinder about 15 inches long. Place 2 cylinders on a lightly greased baking sheet (allow plenty of room between them; the dough will spread somewhat during baking). Refrigerate the remaining strips until ready to shape them.

Bake until golden, about 25 minutes. Let cool, then cut diagonal slices about ¾ inch thick. Spread cookies out on a baking pan, leaving a little space between them. Bake again at 350 degrees for 15 minutes or until toasted. When cool, dip about halfway in melted chocolate. Repeat with remaining dough. Store cookies in airtight tins.

Note: Try to keep the chocolate at 90 degrees while dipping.

PER COOKIE
calories 103 • fat 6g • % calories from fat 52 • saturated fat 2.5g • cholesterol 14mg • protein 1.5g • carbohydrate 11g • sugar 7.5g • fiber 1g • sodium 22mg • calcium 14mg • potassium 54mg

HOUSE OF INDIA 8501 Delmar Boulevard • University City, Mo. • 314-567-6850 • www.hoistl.com

KHEER

Yield: 3 cups

4 cups milk

¼ cup Indian basmati rice, rinsed well and drained

½ teaspoon sliced almonds, plus more for optional garnish

¼ teaspoon ground green cardamom (see note)

¼ cup plus 2 tablespoons granulated sugar

1 teaspoon flaked coconut, plus more for optional garnish

Chopped pistachio nuts, for garnish

Bring milk to a boil over medium heat, watching carefully to prevent boiling over and scorching. Add rice; cook until slightly thickened, stirring frequently, about 20 minutes. Turn off heat. Stir in almonds, cardamom, sugar and coconut.

Serve hot or cold. Garnish with pistachios and, if desired, almonds and coconut.

Note: Only green cardamom, available in many Asian, Indian and natural-food markets, will give the kheer its distinctive fragrance and delicate flavor. (White or black preground cardamom does not have the same scent or flavor.) To grind, place about 5 of the green pods in a mortar and mash with a pestle, or use a glass bowl and the back of a spoon. The small seeds inside can be pulverized easily. Include the green outer shell, which dissolves in the kheer. Prepare only what you need, as the flavor dissipates quickly after grinding.

PER (½-CUP) SERVING
calories 184 • fat 6g • % calories from fat 29 • saturated fat 3.5g • cholesterol 22mg • protein 6g • carbohydrate 26.5g • sugar 20g • fiber 0.5g • sodium 81mg • calcium 195mg • potassium 250mg

CHOCOLATE CHUNK MUFFINS

Yield: 10 Texas-size muffins (see note)

³/₄ cup (1¹/₂ sticks) butter

5¹/₄ cups (1¹/₄ pounds) cake or pastry flour

1 cup minus 1 tablespoon granulated sugar

2 tablespoons baking powder

1¹/₄ teaspoons salt

2 eggs

2 cups milk

1 cup chocolate chunks

3 tablespoons raw sugar, for garnish

Preheat oven to 400 degrees. Generously grease and flour 10 large (about ²/₃-cup) muffin cups. Melt butter; set aside to cool slightly.

In a large bowl, stir together flour, sugar, baking powder and salt. In another bowl, beat eggs until blended; whisk in milk and melted butter. Stir into flour mixture; stir in chocolate chunks. Fill prepared muffin cups about ³/₄ full. Sprinkle with raw sugar. Bake 17 minutes or until a wooden pick inserted in the center comes out clean.

Note: Muffins rise more freely and finish with a better shape if you don't use paper liners. This recipe also makes 20 standard-size muffins; bake about 13 minutes.

PER MUFFIN
calories 543 • fat 21.5g • % calories from fat 36 • saturated fat 13g • cholesterol 83mg • protein 8g • carbohydrate 79.5g • sugar 35g • fiber 2g • sodium 575mg • calcium 225mg • potassium 222mg

GRONE'S CAFETERIA After more than 70 years in business in St. Louis, the Grone family closed the last of their cafeterias in 2004.

ORANGE FLUFF CAKE

Yield: 12 servings

8 eggs, separated

1 1/2 cups granulated sugar

1 teaspoon salt

3/4 cup freshly squeezed orange juice (from 3 to 4 medium oranges), divided

1 1/2 cups sifted cake flour (sift before measuring)

6 teaspoons grated orange zest (colored portion of peel), divided

1 1/4 teaspoons cream of tartar

3 tablespoons butter or margarine, softened

3 cups powdered sugar

Preheat oven to 350 degrees.

Separate eggs into two large bowls. Beat yolks, granulated sugar and salt until light and fluffy. Add 1/2 cup orange juice; continue to beat. Add flour; mix briefly, just until flour is incorporated. Stir in 4 teaspoons zest.

Using clean beaters, beat egg whites until foamy. Add cream of tartar; beat until soft peaks form. Do not overbeat.

Using a rubber spatula, gently fold yolk mixture into whites.

Pour mixture evenly into an ungreased 10-inch tube pan. Bake 35 to 45 minutes or until cake is lightly browned and the center springs back when touched lightly. Remove cake from oven. Invert cake in pan on a rack, the neck of a bottle or the neck of a funnel; let cool completely.

While cake is cooling, prepare icing: In large bowl, combine butter, powdered sugar, remaining 1/4 cup orange juice and remaining 2 teaspoons orange zest. Stir until smooth.

Using a knife, gently separate the cooled cake from the sides of the pan. Invert the cake onto a plate. Frost the top and sides of the cake.

PER SERVING
calories 344 • fat 6g • % calories from fat 16 • saturated fat 3g • cholesterol 149mg • protein 5g • carbohydrate 67.5g • sugar 56g • fiber 0.5g • sodium 245mg • calcium 24mg • potassium 146mg

STICKY TOFFEE PUDDING

Yield: About 18 servings

- **⅓ cup unsalted butter, softened, plus more to prepare pan**
- **1¾ cups all-purpose flour, plus more to prepare pan**
- **8 ounces (1½ packed cups) chopped dried dates**
- **1⅓ cups hot water**
- **1⅓ teaspoons baking soda**
- **1 cup superfine sugar**
- **3 medium eggs**
- **Scant ¾ teaspoon baking powder**
- **Scant ¼ teaspoon salt**
- **Scant ¾ teaspoon vanilla**
- **Caramel Sauce (see recipe)**
- **Whipped cream, for garnish**

Preheat oven to 350 degrees. Grease a 9-by-13-inch baking pan with butter. Coat with flour; shake out excess. Set aside.

Combine dates and hot water in a medium saucepan. Bring to a boil. Remove from heat; add baking soda. Set aside to let cool.

In a large mixing bowl, beat ⅓ cup butter and sugar on high speed for about 3 minutes. With mixer on low speed, add one egg at a time, beating after each addition. When mixture is well-combined, add 1¾ cups flour, baking powder and salt. Add dates and their liquid. Mix well. Add vanilla, stirring just enough to incorporate it.

Pour batter into prepared pan. Bake for 25 to 30 minutes or until the cake is firm and a toothpick inserted near the center comes out clean. Let cool, then cut into serving pieces and remove from pan.

To serve: Warm each serving of cake in a microwave for a few seconds. To serve, top with warm Caramel Sauce and a dollop of whipped cream.

CARAMEL SAUCE

Yield: 4 cups

- **4 cups packed light brown sugar**
- **2 cups (4 sticks) butter**
- **2 teaspoons vanilla**
- **1 cup heavy cream, optional**

Stir together sugar, butter and vanilla over low heat for about 20 minutes, until brown sugar has dissolved and ingredients are well-blended. For a smoother, less grainy sauce, stir in cream. Keep warm until serving time.

PUDDING PER SERVING (without sauce or whipped cream)
calories 168 • fat 4g • % calories from fat 21 • saturated fat 2g • cholesterol 44mg • protein 2.5g • carbohydrate 30.5g • sugar 20g • fiber 1g • sodium 159mg • calcium 25mg • potassium 108mg
SAUCE PER 2-TABLESPOON SERVING
calories 207 • fat 11g • % calories from fat 48 • saturated fat 7g • cholesterol 30mg • protein 0 • carbohydrate 27g • sugar 26.5g • fiber 0 • sodium 12mg • calcium 27mg • potassium 99mg

NERUDA 4 Club Centre Court • Edwardsville, Ill. • 618-659-9866 • www.neruda2dine.com

DARK CHOCOLATE TORTE

Yield: 8 servings

FOR TORTE:

2 cups (4 sticks) unsalted butter

8 ounces semisweet chocolate chips

6 eggs

1 cup granulated sugar

1½ cups unsweetened cocoa powder

FOR GLAZE:

¼ cup (½ stick) unsalted butter

8 ounces milk chocolate

½ cup heavy cream

FOR SERVING:

Fresh raspberries

Raspberry sauce

To prepare torte: Preheat oven to 350 degrees. Lightly grease a 9-inch springform pan.

Combine butter and chocolate chips in a medium saucepan; stir over low heat until melted. Let cool for at least 10 minutes.

Whisk eggs in a large bowl. Gradually whisk in sugar until blended. Gradually whisk in melted chocolate mixture until well blended. Sift cocoa powder; whisk into egg mixture. Pour into the prepared pan; bake 30 to 40 minutes or until firm. Let cool in the pan.

To prepare glaze: In a heavy medium pan, combine butter, milk chocolate and cream. Cook over low heat, stirring gently, until mixture is smooth. Remove springform ring from cake; pour glaze over cake and refrigerate until cold.

To serve: Garnish each slice with fresh raspberries and raspberry sauce.

Tester's note: This recipe does not contain flour. The torte is excellent served cold, as presented at Neruda, but is slightly easier to slice and still tastes great when served cool or at room temperature. Because it is rich, this cake could easily serve 12.

PER SERVING (without garnishes)
calories 1,050 • fat 80g • % calories from fat 69 • saturated fat 48g • cholesterol 345mg • protein 12g • carbohydrate 70.5g • sugar 56g • fiber 6.5g • sodium 94mg • calcium 125mg • potassium 520mg

217

INDEX

APPETIZERS

Balsamic Roasted Portobello
with Brie 35

Blue Cheese Soufflé 13

Crostini with Spanakopita 15

David Slay's Original Crispy
Fried Spinach 19

Grilled Portobellos 33

Mangia Wings in Cayenne
Honey Sauce 23

Pan-Fried Green Olives Stuffed
with Sausage and Herbed
Goat Cheese 21

Shrimp Sambuca 39

Skillet Cornbread
with Rock Shrimp 37

Spinach-Artichoke Dip 17

ARTICHOKES

Artichoke Parmesan Quiche . .61

Chopped Veggie Salad 163

Sautéed Scallops with
Chardonnay Sauce 105

Spinach-Artichoke Dip 17

ASIAN

Green Bean and Mushroom Stir-
Fry (Dau Que Xao Nam) . . .153

Grilled Prairie Grass Farms
Lamb Chops in Asian
Apricot Glaze 129

Sesame Chicken 85

Szechwan Eggplant 151

Thai Red Curry Dragonfly
Pasta 149

BACON

Baked Potato Soup 63

BLT Pasta 137

Corn Chowder 43

BEANS

Green Bean and Mushroom Stir-
Fry (Dau Que Xao Nam) . . .153

White Chili 73

BEEF

Filet Zanti 119

Liver Sweet and Sour 127

Low-Country Meat Pies 123

Mushroom Cheese Steak 121

Steak Salad 115

Tenderloin Spiedini 117

Zuppa per le Feste
(Holiday Soup) 67

BREAD

Brioche Bread Pudding 201

Crostini with Spanakopita 15

Double Chocolate
Bread Pudding 203

Farmhouse Bread 173

French Toast 59

Skillet Cornbread
with Rock Shrimp 37

Sour Cream Blueberry Bread 175

Zucchini Bread 177

BREAKFAST & BRUNCH

Artichoke Parmesan Quiche . .61

Brioche Bread Pudding 201

Farmhouse Bread 173

French Toast 59

Potato 'n' Egg Bake 57

Sour Cream Blueberry Bread 175

Zucchini Bread 177

BROCCOLI

Pasta Con Broccoli 147

CAKE

Bailey's Cheesecake 195

Dark Chocolate Torte 217

Orange Fluff Cake 213

Snickers Cheesecake 197

Sticky Toffee Pudding 215

CARROTS

Chef Hayden's Carrot
Soufflé 169

CHEESE

Artichoke Parmesan Quiche . .61

Baked Potato Soup 63

Balsamic Roasted Portobello
with Brie 35

Barbecued Chicken Pizza 77

Blue Cheese Soufflé 13

Chopped Veggie Salad 163

Crostini with Spanakopita 15

Dock Salsa 27

Filet Zanti 119

Marsala Gorgonzola Cream
Sauce with Polenta Fries . .165

Mushroom Cheese Steak 121

Pan-Fried Green Olives Stuffed
with Sausage and Herbed
Goat Cheese 21

Parmesan-Crusted Sole 97

Pesto Sauce 31

Potato 'n' Egg Bake 57

Spinach-Artichoke Dip 17

Steak Salad 115

Tenderloin Spiedini 117

Tortilla Soup 71

Veal Saltimbocca 125

White Chili 73

Wicklow Salad 51

CHICKEN

Barbecued Chicken Pizza 77

Chickburger 75

Chicken Salad 89

Chicken Valle Douge 79

Grinders 111

Involtini di Petti de Pollo
(Chicken Spiedini) 83

Jambalaya 113

Mangia Wings in Cayenne
Honey Sauce 23

Pollo Agro Dolce (Venetian
Sweet-and-Sour Chicken) . . .81

Red Curry Chicken Salad 87

Sesame Chicken 85

Spicy Sherry-Onion Soup 69

Tortilla Soup 71

White Chili 73

CHOCOLATE

Chocolate-Chip Pie 193

Chocolate Chunk Muffins 211

Chocolate-Dipped Hazelnut
Biscotti 207

Chocolate Pecan Pie 191

Dark Chocolate Torte 217

Double Chocolate
Bread Pudding 203

Snickers Cheesecake 197

Truffle Cookies 205

PHOTO CREDITS